I0834117

Mrs Atterbury

from her affectionate friend

Cornelia A.B. Richards

41 Edmund St

1880

In memory of a

pleasant & profitable summer

C.A.B.R.

Alice B. Haven

# COUSIN ALICE:

A

## MEMOIR OF ALICE B. HAVEN.

NEW YORK:
D. APPLETON AND COMPANY.
549 & 551 BROADWAY.
1871.

TO

THE CHILDREN OF

ALICE B. HAVEN

AND

*TO HER FRIENDS,*

THIS MEMORIAL

OF A LIFE SPENT IN BEARING THE BURDENS OF OTHERS,

AND SO FULFILLING THE LAW OF CHRIST,

IS AFFECTIONATELY

*INSCRIBED.*

"YOU MIGHT HAVE WON THE POET'S NAME
IF SUCH BE WORTH THE WINNING NOW,
AND GAINED A LAUREL FOR YOUR BROW
OF SOUNDER LEAF THAN I CAN CLAIM.

"BUT YOU HAVE MADE THE WISER CHOICE,
A LIFE THAT MOVES TO GRACIOUS ENDS
THROUGH TROOPS OF UNRECORDING FRIENDS
A DEEDFUL LIFE, A SILENT VOICE."

*Tennyson.*

# PREFACE.

THE best words which we can frame to describe a painting by a Master, fall immeasurably below the masterpiece itself in the power of moving the intellect or swaying the feelings of the beholder. Even the silent marble, chiselled into grace and beauty, inspires emotions which are beyond the power of reproduction in the phrases of any language used by one who knows all its secret resources.

Yet these triumphs of art are incommensurable with the moving forms of Beauty and of Grace which they feebly figure and represent. There is hardly more of likeness between them than between death and life. Indeed these are changeless and dead, while that which they embody is changing and vital, whether it be the landscape which is another yet the same, in every hour's sun or shade, in the green of spring or amid the autumn's flying leaves, or whether it be the human form, which with every motion creates a new and livelier sculpture.

There must needs come then to the one who has written, or to them who read, a more painful sense of inadequacy and imperfection, when it is a life which has been portrayed, when it is not the single aspect of a form, or of a scene, but the unfolding and upbuilding of a noble character, which has been attempted to be described; its collision with circumstances, and its inner conflicts. There are even subtler and finer graces in life than in beauty, and a noble character is more indescribable than a splendid view, and less easy to be fixed in any form of words for remembrance or influence, when the scene is distant or the life has been transplanted to another sphere.

Yet it was due that such a life as hers who is the subject of this biography should be written, however briefly or imperfectly; for in the judgment of those who saw merely its spiritual radiance, as well as of those who lived in its life-giving atmosphere, it was a life filled with temptations and trials which wrought in her a singular humility; of afflictions and difficulties converted by a deep religious chemistry into Christian graces; of weaknesses and imperfections transmuted into spiritual symmetry and power. It was a life which none who saw it as it was lived, and none to whom these pages shall convey any just conception of it, would willingly let die.

# CONTENTS.

## PART I.

### *THE ORDEAL.*



## PART II.

### *HOME LIFE.*

## PART III.

### *READY FOR REST.*

## PART I.

# THE ORDEAL.

# PART I.

## *THE ORDEAL.*

---

## CHAPTER I.

### *INTRODUCTORY.*

EMILY BRADLEY was the name borne in childhood by Mrs. Haven. If there is that in blood which particularly forms, or modifies, character, this child had a singular inheritance. Her ancestors, on her father's side, were men whom enterprise and a love of adventure kept upon the sea. Her father's father, and all his brothers, with remoter connections, were sea captains in the various services of our country. They were brave, resolute men, whose determination and daring were proverbial.

Her father, too delicate for such a life, on account of an injury which he had received in his youth, and which prevented his attaining the physical force of his brothers, was yet not unlike them in spirit. Pride, ambition, and indomitable purpose, were the stamina of a character softened by tender and generous impulses. Dying while his four children were all in the years of infancy—even the eldest could only remember him, as a sad-hearted and depressed invalid, consumed by a fiery and hopeless ambition.

He died on the 13th of September, 1830, Emily's third birthday. An infant daughter soon followed the father, and Emily was thus left the youngest of a fatherless group of little ones.

She became the charge of a mother most unlike the father in character and disposition; the representative of a family noted for firm faith and fervent piety. Her maternal ancestry was the counterpart of that on the father's side. Two more opposite races could not have blended. Her mother was of Baptist and Quaker descent. Nearly a score of clergymen could be counted amongst her immediate ancestors and relatives. Her father had had but little sympathy with his wife's family, so unlike himself in traits which, nevertheless, commanded his respect, if they did not arouse his emulation. They were humble-minded, devout, and, in some cases, scholarly men, most unworldly in purpose and unselfish in action. Their strong faith, their unswerving fidelity to their religion, and the simplicity and purity of their lives, sent a sweet and healthful current into the veins of their children.

Emily's largest inheritance, both mental and spiritual, was from this side of the family; but there was a persistent force of character derived from her father, which marked her whole life.

Even in childhood she showed the most opposite traits, one or another predominating in the various phases she passed through, and giving tone to the different periods of her life. These could all be traced in her later years, not then presenting contrarieties that were perplexing and discouraging to those around her, but harmonized by her religion into a character, forcible in action, which was unremitting from principle, and profound in devout meditation, and in a rich, spiritual life. Never was there a better illustration of the many-sidedness which is essential to breadth of interest, sympathy, and purpose. It was this large nature, this comprehensiveness of mind and heart, which, finally, purified by the graces of God's spirit, absorbed self, and made the noble woman.

That this height was not reached without hard struggles, many futile efforts, and much discouragement, by the way, will readily be seen by all who can appreciate the conflicting elements of her nature, the peculiar trials of her life, and a delicate physical constitution, which most persons would have felt justified in pleading as an excuse for many short-comings.

Harmonious character is not an inheritance or an endowment. It is the result of strenuous effort; it is the guerdon of the self-controlled; it is the unconscious crown of the devoted, the self-denying, the resolute and fervent spirit. If intellectual character be "knowledge organized into faculty," then religious character is simple faith matured into spiritual insight.

This child, with her rare endowments, ripened into a woman, illustrating each form of character, while she led a life of increasing singleness and humility.

To trace the growth which had such rich results, and to read from this short life lessons which shall long teach others her sweet wisdom, is our purpose.

## CHAPTER II.

### CHILDHOOD.

FROM an early period a disease of the eyes manifested itself in this child, who had never seemed to promise robust health. This so affected all her school-life, that she was liable to great suffering, yet a peculiar patience under her suffering grew out of it. This was in marked contrast to an elder sister, whose impetuosity often allowed the younger child an ascendency in her superior self-control. There was a difference of five years in their ages; but the difference, even in childhood, was frequently lost sight of in the precocity of Emily and in her early-acquired power of restraint.

She learned so rapidly on all subjects, and every thing that came within her reach, that she was soon noted as a child of rare acquirements. Her memory was as ready as it was retentive; and it was to this faculty that she was indebted for her remarkably extensive knowledge, as her eyes were often useless for months together, for either reading or study.

When she was six years old she was adopted by an uncle, her mother's eldest brother, a clergyman of fine literary taste and scholastic attainment. His wife was a woman of uncommon mental strength, her husband's companion in his library, giving him his best intellectual stimulus and sympathy. This gentleman, the Rev. J. Newton Brown, was residing in Boston at this time, engaged in editing "The Religious Encyclopædia," a work of research and erudition. Mrs. Brown was his constant assistant in the preparation of this book. Though childless, she was a passionate lover of children, finding her recreation in those of her adoption, for another little girl was already sharing the mother's love which overflowed her heart.

They remained in Boston till the work they were engaged upon was completed, and then returned to Exeter, New Hampshire, where Mr.

Brown was a minister of the Baptist church. The time spent in Boston was very pleasant to Emily. The beautiful Common, near which they lived, and where she played, made one of he most cherished pictures in her memory of ner child-life; and associated with it was the fair little Louise, her adopted sister, whom she loved very tenderly.

In Exeter she was able to go to school, as she had done in Boston, for a year or two, when she was attacked by the disease which so often darkened her young life, and which became in this instance a blindness that lasted for several months. That she suffered terribly none could doubt; but her suffering was rarely, if ever, a matter of complaint. She would be patient in a darkened room for hours together, drawing on an imagination and a memory which were equally remarkable, for her pastime. What was read aloud to her she remembered accurately, and she spent a great deal of time in parodying familiar little poems and in composing wonder stories. Sometimes her uncle, who was also an invalid that winter, was her companion, sometimes her elder sister, then living in the family, but oftener the dear little Louise, whose love was a great solace, though the two children were mentally so unlike, that the bond between them was almost entirely that of affection.

Sensitive and imaginative as she was, some idea may be formed of her self-control and patience, from two instances. She bore applications of leeches to her eyelids and face, day after day, for hours at a time, without a perceptible shudder, and with no word of the shrinking which she afterwards declared possessed her to such a degree, that she sometimes thought she should lose her senses.

Another great trial was, that at night she was the only person who slept on that floor of a large three-story house. Her bedroom had been arranged on the first floor, usually occupied by the family during the day, when it was thought she would most need to be surrounded by companions, in the hope that the lone hours which she spent—and these did not begin till the elder members of the family had retired to rest—would be passed by her in sleep. As she never required any thing at night, it was not considered necessary for any one to remain with her.

She said many years afterwards, that no words that she could use, could ever describe the hours of torture she sometimes passed, when suffering or her fears kept her awake, and the victim of her active imagination. She was but nine years old when passing through this ordeal, and few children would have borne it without a murmur, leaving the revelation of her suffering till years had passed.

Her reserve grew upon her, and it was inevitable that she should be easily misunderstood, and should often lack sympathy. This increased the privacy of her inner life, and led her to say frequently that she passed two childhoods equally real, one that all knew of, and another that no one suspected. Traits were manifested in her outward life, giving rise to many fears on the part of those who had charge of her, which gradually gave way to the inner growth out of which the woman was born.

When Emily was nine years old, her own mother was married a second time. The child had always yearned for her own home and the indulgence of that first-remembered mother's love. She and her sister returned in the spring of 1838 to Hudson, N. Y., which was their birthplace and their mother's residence. After spending the summer with her mother, the elder sister, whose school education was in progress, returned to the uncle and aunt, under whose fostering care she remained till her marriage, which occurred as soon as she graduated at school. Mr. Brown was now professor in a theological institution at New Hampton, N. H. There was a young ladies' school in the same town, which had a great reputation then, and here, when Cornelia left, Emily came to pass her girlhood, and receive her mental training.

The two sisters were thus parted; nor were they ever together again except for a few weeks or months, and after the lapse of long intervals of time. Yet as years went by, and like tastes and principles assimilated very unlike natures, the love which never failed between them led to mutual influence, and this to a bond stronger than mere kinship involved.

The school-life of Emily, in Hudson, has its record in a journal begun when she was but twelve years old, and in many little stories written for juvenile magazines and readers. "Keeping a Journal," a story to be found in a little volume, recently published, called "The Pet Bird, and Other Stories, by Cousin Alice," gives the history of the beginning of this first journal and of her practice, which she kept up as long as she lived.

An instance may find place here of her singular patience under disappointment and suffering. Cornelia was married when Emily was thirteen, and spent a few weeks in Hudson with her family, before leaving for the South, where her husband resided.

Various excursions were planned, in which Emily took great delight. The most charming of all was to be a visit paid to a favorite uncle living near the blue range of the Catskills, which bounded the landscape west of the pretty little city of Hudson. This range of mountains had been fertile in romance to the poetic nature of the child. To penetrate them had been a day-dream for years, and now it was to be a reality. She could hardly wait for the morning to come when the journey was to begin; and an enthusiasm, all the more fervent that it was commonly so pent up, was for once poured out in eager expressions of anticipation.

The morning came, golden with promise for the day, when this journey was to begin; but the poor little girl was found quite blind upon the couch to which she had gone the night before so gay with hope. Her brother and sister stood sorrowfully beside her, ready to give up the visit thus saddened by her disappointment, and looking for a lamentation proportioned to the anticipation she had been indulging.

But there were no tears and no murmurings; there was little indication of the sharp pain of body and mind to which they must leave her. She said, simply, "I ought not to have anticipated so much. I should have remembered how liable I am to such attacks as these. This is a common thing with me. Don't think any more of it, or of how much I wanted to go. It will spoil your visit, and that would be worse than losing mine."

Even while she spoke in calm, low tones, her slender little fingers were clasped so forcibly, as to send the blood to their tips, and to show at what a cost she had attained this self-control.

And this was the child's philosophy taught her through much suffering, giving her a power of endurance which, when the grace of God aided and enhanced it, made up the strength of her life.

## CHAPTER III.

*SCHOOL LIFE.*

SOON after the incident just mentioned, Emily went to New Hampton "to complete her education," as the phrase is. She had already exhibited some ambition to become a scholar, and had begun to use her pen, as was shown by an accumulation of manuscripts, some indicating more than common promise, while others were merely the safety-valves of a nature that found little, and inadequate, expression to those around her.

Emily was a member of her uncle's family while she attended school, having the advantage of his supervision of her studies, and of his large and well-selected library. He was a poet himself, and this was also an advantage to the aspir ing girl. But one hindrance always awaited her in the progress she aimed to make. The affection of her eyes subjected her to constant depression, and forbade her taking that place in her classes which she might otherwise have held with ease. She was not infrequently entirely dependent for her preparation for school on the studying aloud of a classmate; and thus prepared, she would still appear to better advantage than many who had been able to spend hours over their books. In a record made in her journal at this time, she says:

"Ill, ill, ill. What is the use of my good resolutions about system and time, and doing my best? Am I never to be perfectly well? Shall I never have what people call health? This thought is enough to wear me out. They say I have *patience!* They little know how terribly I feel the sting of an incurable malady. Am I yet to be entirely blind? But I have seen the time when I thought I could bear even blindness, so the love of God was mine. Now I am without God and without hope."

"To hide my wretchedness, I often assume an ugly manner, and people say, 'how unamiable!'"

"This bitterness must be overcome. It will poison my life."

Expressions like these abound in the pages of her journal.

The reference to her willingness to bear even blindness, if she could feel the support of God's love, will be better understood by an explanation of her state of mind in regard to religion. The child of many prayers, and of vivid spiritual impressions from her earliest years, she had persuaded herself, when only thirteen years old, that she was a fit subject for church membership—and encouraged in this feeling by some who thought her uncommon maturity should be respected in the matter, she had been admitted as a member of the Baptist church in Hudson. As she grew older, and had a clearer perception of what such a step involved, she became aware of her unfitness for the relation, and grew impatient of its restraints, and of the false position in which it placed her.

It had not the effect which such a misstep sometimes has on a young person, who, feeling that she has been the victim of a delusion, fancies that all professing Christians are either victims or impostors. There was never any tendency to scepticism in her mind. She recognized only her own unfitness; and there are continual expressions even in her lightest moods, of dissatisfaction with herself on this account, and of the yearning for something better and higher, and more satisfying than any thing she could yet grasp. In all this she saw only one source of comfort—*the love of God;* and this seemed to be denied to her, though to possess it she thought she would even be willing "to forever close her eyes to every object of beauty and affection," as she says, with great earnestness. She was not apt to give expression to her affection for others in the caressing ways which are natural to some young girls, but her heart was warmer than her manner indicated. She writes of this:

"I have never known positive happiness. My sorrow is all regret, my joy is hope. I live only in the past and future. Often my heart is full of love—love to all around me, even to those whom I treat with apparent coldness and indifference. I cannot let those I love, know it by outward signs, still less by words. Few understand me. I do not quite understand myself, I think."

A few days later appears a record, which gives a rare insight into her nature, and the phase of her life then passing:

"Of all my wild and ambitious dreams, I have never dared commit one to paper; but to-day I am too full of them to repress the thoughts which are crowding upon me.

"I sometimes feel that I am not born for a common destiny, that I have talents which might elevate me above those with whom I now associate—most of them, I mean. I dare not say that I have *genius.* It is too holy a word to be taken lightly. But hundreds have had these same thoughts and feelings, have felt this same spirit strive within them, have hoped, dreamed, prayed, and—died, leaving the world nought with which to keep 'their memories green.' The grave has closed over their high hopes. And this is not all. These persons *have* had genius; outward circumstances alone have hindered its development.

"Then many have been deluded, who have vainly dreamed that they were of the chosen few destined to immortality; and when these dreams have passed away, they have sunk to the common level, content with the common lot. For this reason I have never put my hopes and fears upon paper. I would not care so much for the first fate. I could at least *carry my high thoughts with me;* but the *last*, after all I had hoped, and dreamed, and toiled for, to give up voluntarily, to forget that I ever wished to be distinguished, or to look on those wishes, if remembered, only as the follies of a child—aye more, to be content with this, and to pass through life unnoticed and unknown—this I cannot endure. I am excited this morning. If I waited till my thoughts cooled, I should not place them on record; but, feeling as I now do, I would say, 'henceforth, ambition, be thou my angel!'

"And I would that it might be a holy ambition; that I might have the love of the good as well as the worldly; that I might have the thanks of my fellow-creatures, as well as their praises. Is this a vain dream? *It shall not be.* By a fixed determination, and by every effort, I will accomplish the task I would mark out for myself. For help in this, I look to my journal. I will begin my work by improving my time, and by being ambitious in small things. I will strive to perform my *duty*, and when I come to the great struggle, I shall not be faint-hearted. I cannot afford to waste time now in dreams of what may befall me."

During the years of her school life, this journal is a record of variations of the feeling here described. A thirst for love, which often took the form to those about her of a craving for praise and admiration; a sense of great and increasing dissatisfaction with herself, and in all, by which she vainly sought to alleviate this thirst of her soul; an ambition for a recognition in the region of intellectual producers, and resolves that sustained her even under the greatest discouragements.

She shrunk from revealing her profounder emotions, and did herself great injustice by their concealment. Even to her sister she writes, in the very year in which she makes a record of her resolution to do *duty* well:

> "Your eternal monotone of duty disenchants me with life. Say it is *duty*, and the fire goes out, the living impulse is dead. I hate the word. I was never appealed to by an action that was the offspring of a sense of duty."

It was the struggle of a young and active spirit, feeling its strength "with the sense of wings," but ignorant as yet that strength, to be power, must come under the dominion and into the obedience of law.

Her reserve was, however, sometimes thrown off, and her nobler nature found irresistible expression. A schoolmate, who was in the same family, and her constant companion, bears witness to the rare occasions of which this could be said:

> "I used to sit at her feet and listen to her eloquent words, till I was carried out of the realities of our lives into the higher regions which she seemed to penetrate. I listened in wonder and full faith, and I half worshipped her, as she bore me along. I can never describe the

effect of these talks upon me: they opened new worlds to me. When I used to write to my mother so admiringly of Emily, she, seeing her only as she was commonly known and understood, would rebuke me for yielding myself so much to her influence. But I was borne along by the irresistible force of her genius. People have called her brilliant and fascinating in society since then, and we have heard how unequalled she was in conversational power. Was it strange that I yielded to the power which even then was hers whenever she chose to use it? It was her genius which gave it to her as much then as later in life."

She was herself becoming conscious of the brilliant faculty which afterwards characterized her in society. She was also finding out that she possessed some personal graces, which had their influence on others. Notwithstanding the weakness to which they were liable, her eyes were remarkably beautiful; large, soft, lustrous brown eyes, with a capacity for expression that amounted to fascination. A delicate, well-formed mouth, with the flexible upper lip, which is always attractive: a profusion of rich brown hair, a brilliant color and a graceful bearing, were her chief charms. Her hand was as diminutive as a child's; indeed she required a smaller glove than any ladies' size—her fingers taper and white, and pink-tipped; they certainly did not seem made for life's uses. She used to say laughingly of herself, that her vanity in her hands survived all other weaknesses of the kind; that even when the gravest cares of her later years were resting upon her, her one temptation in dress was fresh and pretty gloves; to these she always treated herself when any pecuniary success made her elate; but she said, "I never wear new gloves to church—I feel so very silly in my consciousness there of my vanity."

This personal vanity was a great trial and temptation, and, finally, mortification to her; but it opened to her one gate to the lovely humility of her later years. In her girlhood it was indulged, as would be natural to one who was admired and flattered. She did not think she was beautiful even in later life, when "her features had been chiselled by thought," but she felt that she had personal power, especially in her conversation with men, and she involuntarily exulted in it, always to follow it with a self-inflicted humiliation, which a sense of the pettiness of the pleasure brought her. She did not attempt to analyze the power she possessed, but to exercise it was a temptation few of her age could have resisted. Against this exercise, however, she was soon on her guard, and very early we find her making resolutions to refrain from it, and to live down with nobler aims the consciousness which might become the bane of her life.

The more intense her dissatisfaction with herself, the more trifling and reckless was her bearing to those who sought to do her good. She writes:

"This spirit of evil will alienate all my friends. I see their discouragement; I hear their predictions of evil for me; I know their distrust of my motives, and their want of comprehension of me—their lack of appreciative sympathy makes me desperate. I seize the present good, and let them croak on, while God only knows how miserable I am, and how I hate myself for this double life, this denial of the good which is contending with the evil of my nature."

One of her teachers, a close observer and good student of human nature, wrote to her sister:

"Emily gives me many anxious hours. She lacks heart; she lacks the power to rise above herself, and to forget herself in the happiness and good of others. I am compelled to fear, too, that she is wanting in principle. She is not frank; and when I am talking with her, I am conscious that her soul is veiled to me. One day she said, in a cold, sarcastic tone, after an hour of remonstrance on my part: 'I thank you for your good intentions. You are, however, very unjust to me—but I am used to that, and can bear it. I am thankful for one faculty—the power to hold my tongue when words would not avail.' Thus buffeted back, what can I do for her? Yet she has an extraordinary mind; she is mentally fascinating, and will be so externally. She is proudly ambitious; and should she continue so, and ever have good health and the untrammelled use of her eyes, she will not rest till she has achieved a reputation as a writer. I must believe that she wears the worst outside, that she is much better at heart than she is willing to have us believe. I once heard her say: 'Above all things, I hate cant. What my life does not do for me in commanding the respect of others, may go undone. I cannot talk *goodey*.'"

## CHAPTER IV.

### *HER MARRIAGE.*

' For a wonder-change within her heart,
At that sweet time is wrought,
When on the heart is softly laid
The spell of deeper thought."

THIS is inscribed at the beginning of the last volume which records her school life, and if the writer could have anticipated all the book would hold, it could not have had a fitter preface. Thought and feeling were working "wonder changes" during these moulding years. Externally, there was a life of feverish excitement, contrasting with the despondencies her ill health could not fail to bring. Emily, as she said of herself afterwards, went to her journal as to a confessional, and it bears witness now of the sharp struggle which her noble aspirations had with the temptations to levity and frivolity that so often gained the victory at that period. No one could condemn her failures so severely as she condemns them herself, and constantly she vows herself to a higher life, in whose serene atmosphere of self-denial and worthy purpose she should be able to command her self-respect. Her standard was never lowered, but her lips were continually false to the nobility of her soul, and that she so misrepresented herself, filled her with remorse.

The books she read, the criticisms she has recorded of them, and the books and poems she planned and, in some cases, began, show how unflagging was her mental activity. There are graphic sketches and fine plans for poems, and even dramas of an ambitious sort, introduced from time to time—ending generally with a sigh over her inadequacy to their accomplishment. Her contributions to the school literature, and the essays, sketches, or poems which she read before its "Literary Society," were original and full of promise. Those who were appreciative amongst the teachers, and her maturer friends, already predicted for her a brilliant literary career. *They did not foresee that this strong, personal ambition, would merge, as her heart expanded and her life developed, into nobler purposes and loftier aims, to whose accomplishment she would sacrifice every personal advantage and every thought of self.*

During part of her last term at school, she occupied herself with a travesty of the fourth book of the Æneid, which was very cleverly done, and which was read with great applause at a public examination. Even at this age she was fitted for such a work by a quick and subtle play of humor, joined to a fine, keen wit. These qualities gave piquancy to the expression of the most commonplace ideas, and aided always in the brilliant effect of her conversation. No good point in a subject escaped her, and her use of language was dextrous and graceful. She lacked, of course, the finish which came later, but her power of expression was remarkable notwithstanding this. In conversation, her repartee, which flashed as quickly, and in those days not as innocently, as the summer lightning, the ready allusion for which she was indebted to her memory, the apt quotation from the same source, the witty comparison so clever, and yet so unexpected by slower and less fertile minds, made up the quality of the talk, which came with feminine fluency, and in a low, soft voice, whose pretty inflections were always attractive in themselves.

A friend, rising one day to say farewell, gave it with a graceful quotation. Catching up his idea, she poured out quotation after quotation for at least ten minutes, till it seemed as if she had exhausted all applicable passages in the familiar poets, and then she said, "I only stop for want of breath." "I believe you," was the reply; "you would do for a poetical dictionary."

The writer recalls an instance of her uncommon memory. It occurred some years after, when she was living in Philadelphia. They were spending the day together, and Emily said,

"Have you seen 'In Memoriam' yet?"

"No, though very impatient for my first reading."

"So am I; I will send and get the book."

The book was brought, and she began to read aloud. As she read, her heart and eyes were full, for she had now entered upon her sad experience of bereavement. When she finished reading, she closed the book, and, referring to some passages so beautiful, that they had been twice read, she repeated them, and without re-opening the volume, she recalled other passages that had struck her, and continued this till she had repeated more than half the poem, and then stopped because visitors were announced.

"And you have never seen this book till this morning?" said her listener, with great surprise.

"Certainly I have not. And now you see to what I am indebted for most that I know, learned in spite of my eyes."

It was not verse only, where the rhyme and rhythm are so helpful to the memory, that she thus kept in mind, nor that alone which appealed to her imagination and tastes. Strange as it may seem, she had a great fondness for statistical information, and a masculine grasp of ideas that one would never suppose would find place in her mind. She was greedy of such knowledge, and listened eagerly to any one from whom it could be gathered. After her editorial life began, this was manifest. A review of a volume on Political Economy fell from her pen before her cheek had lost its girlish bloom, and she wrote innumerable articles on subjects women rarely touch, even in their reading. Had her eyes allowed her opportunity for thorough study, the vigor of her intellect would have been as eminent as its grace. Every year of her life gave some evidence of this.

She had a great desire to be a good musician, but she never had strength to spend that time at the piano which was necessary to her becoming a fine *executante.* This was a constant pain to her. Her voice was sweet, but lacked power. She sung charmingly, however, accompanying herself, and often adapted music to words. She delighted in minor music, and had a peculiar taste in songs. In her young days she sung very archly and with much variety of expression; later in life, singing was *worship* to her, and she gave preference to sacred pieces. The last song she ever sung, and her favorite for years, was a little poem, "The Two Brides," by R. H. Stoddard, set to a weird tune, which haunted all who heard it.

She made frequent contributions, while at school, to the papers and magazines of the day.

This displeased her friends, who were desirous that she should not publish till her powers were more mature. Her sister wrote to her from the South, asking that she should not see her name before the public till she had reached the age of eighteen. The request was literally complied with, but her contributions were sent as formerly, only under feigned names. The popularity of a poem written when she was sixteen, and copied into more than thirty journals, made the temptation to publish too strong to be resisted. These lines are a fair expression of that period. They were suggested by a sentence in Bulwer's play of *Richelieu*—"In the bright lexicon of youth there is no such word as *fail.*" And this poem, part of which is copied here, is also a school-girl's production, and seems to give voice to the aspiration which marked her true inner life. The motto is from another poem:

"It is not the dream of a fancy proud,
With a fool for its dull begetter,
A voice *from the spirit* proclaims aloud,
*We are born for something better.*"

And hast thou, too, been pining long
For that which may not be?
Dost thou share in the solemn thoughts
That long have dwelt with me?

Thy words have wakened once again
  The wish within my heart,
That in a nobler, freer life,
  My spirit might have part.

I strove to check my soaring thoughts,
  And turned once more to earth,
Seeking in pleasure to forget
  The mood that gave them birth.

But now they cast aside the chain,
  And, spurning all control,
Bid that I listen, and obey
  The voice within my soul.

I know when comes the spell on thee,
  When from thy weakness bowed,
The tide that ebbed within thy heart
  Flows once more strong and proud.

When thou wouldst strive to rend the bonds
  That fetter thee, and find
New life, where *custom* leadeth not,
  Where forms no longer bind—

The earth is then a mockery;
  Existence but a dream;
And those who share with thee its fears,
  As shadowy phantoms seem.

When space, infinity alone,
  Seems vast enough to fill
The void which, struggle as thou wilt,
  Dwells in the bosom still.

* * * * * *

These are but dreams—we are of earth,
  And here we must abide;
Must quell, subdue, these murmurings,
  And check this daring pride.

Our spirits are too gross, too dark,
  In such a land to be,
And from the bonds of earth and sin
  By death alone made free.

Yet when through gloom, and gathering storms,
  The vale of death is passed,
When from this vesture of decay
  The soul is free at last;

When sweeping pinions unto us
  With boundless strength are given,
Then shall we know this purer life,
  As found alone in Heaven."

At this time Joseph C. Neal, of Philadelphia, the author of "Charcoal Sketches," which were then in the height of their popularity, retired from the editorship of the "Pennsylvanian," and established a literary newspaper, which he called "Neal's Saturday Gazette." Some numbers of this paper found their way to New Hampton, and excited the admiration of the clique in school who aspired to be writers.

Emily having carelessly remarked that this

would be a good paper in which to appear, was challenged by her companions to find admittance to its columns. Accepting the challenge, she wrote a story called "The First Declaration," which she sent to Mr. Neal with the *nom de plume* of ALICE G. LEE, using a middle name, Gordon, to make the incognito more complete. The story was not only accepted, but was published, with a very kind editorial notice, in which Mr. Neal says:

> "Though second to none in our admiration of Fanny Forrester, it would be injustice not to say that "The First Declaration" will compare, without injury, with any production of the kind that has of late adorned our periodical literature. How it affects others we cannot tell; but it is to us like moonlight on the flowers when the weary day is done, or like music on the water, to meet with a sketch so replete with playfulness, yet so delicately marked with Coleridge's 'instinct of ladyhood.' There is genius, too, and originality in its naiveté; a nice and feminine perception of the beautiful, with an ability to portray it, which cannot fail of its purpose whenever it is exercised."

Such commendation from such a source was an inspiration to the ambitious girl; and of course this contribution was followed by others, both prose and verse, many of which were kindly alluded to by Mr. Neal in his "Notices to Correspondents."

In the course of the summer Emily left school for her home in Hudson. There, in the autumn, a correspondence sprung up between Mr. Neal and herself. It originated in a request which she made, when sending him something for his paper, that he would be good enough to give her his real opinion of her writings. She says she made the request with much hesitation, and after the letter was sent off would gladly have recalled it. But he responded at once, and so kindly, yet critically, that she received the best sort of encouragement. She continued to write freely, but did not publish every thing; indeed, from this time Mr. Neal exercised a most friendly supervision over her mental progress, for their letters were soon numerous, and his were expressive of an increasing interest.

One tendency in her mind which was evident in her writing, and for which she certainly had singular talent, was to show up the weak points of others, and to expose the social fictions which she encountered in her first entrance into society.

Her unlikeness in tastes and pursuits to those with whom she associated, the admiration she easily won, and her indifference to conventional exactions, had the effect of calling forth some strictures in the little town, which she met with keen sarcasm; and she thus gathered material for some stories, in which was the germ of the volume she published a few years after, called "The Gossips of Rivertown."

A story in this vein was sent to Mr. Neal that winter, but he delayed its publication, and used his influence to show her that she would find the indulgence of such a spirit a bane to her powers. She describes her usual mood from fourteen to twenty as very morbid; and it was not strange that a root of bitterness should take hold in the rank growth which resulted from the circumstances of her life. She appreciated the kindness of the strictures made by her wise friend; her heart taught her that she was not elevating herself by such indulgence, and she willingly refrained from the use of her powers of irony and sarcasm, cultivating instead charity toward others, pity for their faults of ignorance and narrowness, and a strong perception of the good in all, of the beautiful everywhere.

It was quite a year from the time her first story had attracted his attention, and after their correspondence had assumed somewhat of an intimate character, that Mr. Neal was informed of the real name of his young protégée. Before this time, Emily had written to her sister of the discomfort she was beginning to feel in her incognito. In seeking once to account for his interest in her, he had said, pleasantly, "Perhaps your name has something to do with it. *Alice Gordon Lee* sounds very Scotch, and my mother is a Scotchwoman, you know." That she was awakening a personal interest could not be unfelt, and she began to wish the deception was ended.

At this time, a young gentleman friend, a cadet at West Point, returned to that place at the expiration of a furlough, and wrote to Mr. Neal to have the "Gazette" sent to him again, saying, "It has a new charm for me now, since I find it contains the contributions of a dear friend, under the *nom de plume* of Alice G Lee." Mr. Neal was very much surprised, and wrote a witty letter to the young lady who had so long and so successfully worn the mask.

Having made acquaintance while he was passing through Philadelphia with Emily's brother-in-law, Mr. Richards, who was also an editor, at the South, Mr. Neal proposed to visit him in Hudson, where Mrs. Richards had been spending the summer with her mother and sister. The visit was made in September, 1846. It resulted in a confirmation of the agreeable impression their letters had produced; and on his return to Philadelphia, Mr. Neal wrote, declaring his affection for the brilliant young girl, whose ability he had admired and fostered, and offering marriage. He was accepted, and the wedding-day was fixed in the coming December.

As the time for the marriage drew near, Emily was violently attacked by the disease which had so long affected her eyes, and lay for some time dangerously ill with erysipelas in the head. On learning her danger Mr. Neal came to Hudson immediately, and remained with her till she was able to leave as his wife.

From this time her eyes were quite well; this violent manifestation of the malady ending the suffering which, from the time of her third year, had been so frequent and so unmanageable. At last she could comprehend more nearly than ever before "what people call health," though she was not even now to know it always, for from this time she became a victim to nervous headaches, which, while she accounted them slight suffering when compared to that she had been accustomed to, most persons are willing to make an excuse for the indulgences of the invalid.

# CHAPTER V.

## *THE YOUNG WIFE.*

A NEW volume of the journal begins the record of her new life. On its first page is a motto from Burns, whose significance was made plain by the events which followed her removal to Philadelphia.

> "Who made the heart, 'tis He alone
> Decidedly can try us,
> He knows each chord, its various tone,
> Each spring, its various bias;
> Then at the balance, let's be mute,
> We never can adjust it,
> What's done we partly may compute,
> But never what's resisted."

Below this are Mrs. Fry's rules for daily living:

"1. Never lose any time. I do not think that lost which is spent in amusement or recreation some time every day; but always be in the habit of being employed.

"2. Never err the least in truth.

"3. Never say an ill thing of a person when thou canst not say a good thing of him. Not only speak charitably, but *feel* so.

"4. Never be irritable or unkind to any one.

"5. Never indulge thyself in luxuries that are not necessary.

"6. Do all things with consideration; and when thy path to right action is most difficult, feel confidence in the Power which alone is able to assist thee, and exert thy own powers as far as they go."

Thus did she begin to hedge up her way to the exercise of faulty propensities, and to signify the fresh and worthy aims of her life.

Mr. Neal was an only child, and resided with his widowed mother. To this home he brought his young wife, introducing her to one who was to exert no little influence on her mind and character. Mrs. Neal was about seventy then; but though her fragile form showed the infirmities of age, her dignified bearing and her clear and vigorous intellect made it plain that such a companion must be of unspeakable advantage to the daughter-in-law. Scotch by birth, as her son had said of her, her life from her early widowhood had been devoted to the rearing of her son. For forty years she had been his best friend and adviser. In his literary life she had kept pace with him; she was not only at home in modern literature, but familiar with old English and classic stores. A ripe scholar, her mind yet untouched by the blight of age, a severe yet not unkindly critic, as elevated as she was clear and vigorous—could the young writer have had a better companion, or come under more favorable influences?

It was a trying ordeal for an inexperienced girl, such an entrance into society. Her husband's friends were naturally men and women of cultivated and mature intellects, who had their own misgivings of the fitness of a marriage of such unequal ages and natures. All were kind to the blooming girl who came like sunshine into the quiet household; all whom nature had endowed with a perception of the trials before her, and who saw what was hidden from her in the future.

At the request of Mr. Neal, and his mother also, "Alice" became the household name of the bride, and known only by this in the circle of her new friends, and to the public, before whom she appeared more frequently now as a writer, her real name fell quite into disuse. She wrote so much that first year, that then, and for some time after, she used other cognomens for the reading world—that of "Clara Cushman" was almost as well known as Alice G. Lee.

It was over this signature that she wrote a graceful little story, called "The Chapel Bell." She had been saying to Mr. Neal that imitation of the German, and indeed other foreign tongues, was less difficult than one imagined. She fancied *she* could enter into the spirit of the German at least, well enough to deceive the public. He bade her try, and the little story which she prefaced with "Translated from the German," was the result. How well she succeeded may be inferred from the fact, that John G. Saxe, struck by the poetic beauty of the sketch, turned it into rhyme, calling it "a paraphrase from the German." He was not aware that he was under any illusion in regard to it, till Alice's brother-in-law called attention in his paper to the sketch as originally published in "Neal's Gazette." It had then appeared in a collection of Mr. Saxe's poems, and had been pronounced by a reviewer the most poetical in spirit of any thing Mr. Saxe had ever written!

The poet at once made a courteous and graceful acknowledgment to Mrs. Neal of his indebtedness to her, and subsequent editions of his poems contain the same acknowledgment in a note appended to the poem in question.*

This and some other things very unlike each other in character, were written at her husband's suggestion, that she might try her wings. He was confident of her ability, and proud of it, and his aim was to give it a symmetrical development and thorough culture.

Under date of February 15th, 1847, Alice writes in her journal:

"I know that I was born to do good, and that not in a narrow circle. Even my husband does not understand this ambition which fills my heart. He says, 'all young

---

* "This ballad is a paraphrase of a beautiful prose tale written by Mrs. Alice B. Neal, and published as a translation 'from the German.' The story is so extremely 'Germanesque' in its style and spirit, that the best scholars in the country did not suspect its American origin, till the fact was recently disclosed by a relative of the gifted authoress."

people are ambitious; it is characteristic of their age.' He is mistaken, I trust. This strange impulse for an extended sphere of action, which seems at last working to an end, is not a childish whim. I am strong, though they do not know it—strong alike for good or evil. It had nearly been evil, but, thank God, that mood has departed I am learning daily, grasping more and more that is to be of use to me in the future: storing material for labor that is to come."

But it was not all work and study. This was her first experience of a life whose glimpses heretofore had only tantalized her. The new world of music, opened to her in the opera and concert-room, she entered with the zest of a first love. Histrionic art fascinated her. The brilliant conversation of the clever and cultivated friends of Mr. Neal, in which he shone so preëminently, was always delightful to her. She found her husband loved and honored, and her pride as well as her love was satisfied. She never wearied of watching the impression he produced; her own was always of secondary interest. He was a man of delicate mould and organization, with sweet and noble features and most intellectual head, fair, waving hair, and soft blue eyes. His voice was low and well-modulated; his conversation was distinguished by humor rather than wit. This most winning and amiable nature was so well understood generally, that, though for thirteen years the editor of a leading daily political paper, he might be said to be without an enemy in the world! The lash which he was so capable of using, was applied with such dexterity and rare judgment, that those who suffered were at the same time shown their error, and compelled to acknowledge that justice had overtaken them. His heart always held his pen on the line where judgment and mercy met.

He was, as before their marriage, Alice's most competent teacher, and best intellectual guide. Her appreciation of this, and her acknowledgment during all her life of her indebtedness to him, made a tie between them as strong and beautiful as the romance of their love. She bent herself to improvement with all assiduity, now that opportunity was so rich for it. In character her gain was as great as the development was rapid. She combated diligently with faults, the result of nature, and the growth of her girlhood's suffering. She writes:

"My besetting sins now are indolence and irresolution. 'I will do so much to-morrow, or next week.' To-morrow comes and is gone; week after week passes, and I am planning rather than executing. My bane has always been a consciousness of ability, and impatience of feeble results. Thus I am easily discouraged and despondent. What I have done is a small part of what I can do."

When they had been married three or four months Mr. Neal had a peculiar illness, resembling brain fever. There was always danger with him, from his delicate physical organization, of brain trouble, the mental development being very disproportionate. From the prostration of the fever he recovered; and though to the casual acquaintance he seemed quite well again, yet the balance was never restored. On some subjects a settled mania continued, and there were intervals when reason was quite unseated.

How Alice bore herself in this terrible trial, must be gathered from two records—one made in her journal, and the other in a note addressed by Mr. Neal to her sister, under date of May 13th. She writes:

"My journal has always been a solace; may it be so now, for truly I have need of a comforter. When I commenced this volume I was full of hope; a new day, the brightest of my life, was dawning. Now it would seem as though hope had forever left me. My husband is, I fear, incurably insane; a fate more terrible than my imagination could have pictured. God only knows what he is suffering. I, his wife, who am with him night and day, cannot tell a tithe of the agony which makes him weary of life.

"'It is hard to leave you, my own Alice,' he says; 'I dare not think of the parting with my poor mother. Yet would that I might end my despair; would that I could sleep in peace.'

"And then he reproaches himself for bringing me from a happy home to a scene of so much present and future misery. In vain I tell him that I have strength 'to hope all things, suffer all things;' that I know he will recover. 'Every dark cloud has its silver lining,' I say. This is, perhaps, but the shadow of that dreaded 'first year,' of which we often spoke.

"'Poor child,' he replies; 'would to heaven it were so for your sake and my poor mother's. Oh, Alice, that you should love me so well! Promise me the day shall never come when you will curse my memory, when you will say, "he was the destroyer of my peace."'

"My husband! would to God that I could die for thee! Perhaps I do not know my own heart, but now I feel sure that I could die calmly and happily, did I know that my death would restore to him health and happiness.

"Most terrible of all—none but myself know the fatal secret. I must bear my fear and its anguish alone.

"I knew I was *too* happy—that some fearful gloom was hanging over that bridal—even though my heart fainted with excess of joy.

"I will try to banish this fear. It may be that we are both deceived; that my husband will yet be restored to me.

"'Father, if it be possible, let this cup pass from me.'"

In the note to his sister-in-law, Mr. Neal writes:

"I intend this missive as a humble companion to the more extended remarks and observations of my good and dear Alice, wishing to say to you that she makes the best of wives, and especially as regards good temper, an accommodating spirit, and very great forbearance, which perhaps may a little surprise you, as she has been terribly tried by my affliction, which has been a long, protracted illness of a singular character. Give her credit, then, as I do, for the exercise of the most Christian virtues, and love her more for the bright traits of character which trial has educed, perhaps as much to her own surprise as to the gratification of others."

Two or three months more went by, and the troubled spirit of Joseph C. Neal was at rest. He died suddenly, and just as his friends, and even himself, had begun to hope that the cloud might be lifted, and his mind restored to perfect serenity. He was quite conscious of his condition during intervals of more or less length; and, as the preceding extracts have shown, talked of it with his wife, and understood and loved her the more tenderly for the strength and deepening love which his situation created in her.

But at last the silver cord was loosed; the beautiful mind was no more shrouded in the clouds which the suffering body cast over it, and the gentle and loving heart lost its pain as it grew cold in death.

The aged mother lost the object of a life's devotion; the young wife, one whom she reverenced and loved with the fervor and romance of her age and nature. They clasped their arms about each other, and resolved henceforth to abide together in the home made sacred to both by the memories of their beloved. In their agony they were yet not uncomforted. for it had been made plain to them that his life would never again be unclouded, and they knew the time might come when they would both covet for him the repose of the grave.

## CHAPTER VI.

### *THE FIRST YEAR OF WIDOWHOOD.*

THERE is no record immediately following Mr. Neal's death. Alice was long recovering from the shock. The strain upon her nervous system could not but be severely felt for many months, and the bewildering effects of her sudden bereavement were almost paralyzing. But the record made on her next birthday will tell the story better:

"Sept. 13th, 1847.

"My twentieth birthday, so long looked forward to, finds me a childless widow. It is nearly two months since my poor husband was laid at rest, free from mental suffering! free from fear of death! 'He may not come to me, but I shall go to him.'

"Thanks and great glory to the Heavenly Father,

who has given me strength to bear the sharp and won derful trials of the past year; who has given me peace of mind and resignation under this severest of earthly afflictions. I, too, should have gone mad if I could not have prayed, if I had not the knowledge that He orders all things for my good. There seems to be a direct message from Him, to tell me that henceforth my life must be devoted to His service.

"A few days after my husband's death, I entered the little study where we had so often read together. The Life of Madame Guyon was lying on the table. Scarce knowing what I did, I opened it, as the thought came to me that this was the last book he had spoken to me about. We were, I am grieved to say it, laughing at what we thought her fanaticism, as it regarded her faith in special interpositions of Providence in her behalf.

"How kindly, yet how terribly, was God about to manifest the truth of this to me!

"I opened the book at random, and my eyes fell upon a passage that described my feelings exactly. I felt in an instant that I was directed to its reading, and I prayed that God would receive me as His child, and from that moment would mould me to His will. I remembered that it was just a year from the hour when I had made a similar prayer and resolve. Then I had just heard of my poor Louise's death, my first great earthly loss. I do think that God has had me in His special keeping since that time I have been led away from my resolve by my peculiar position during the past winter, and have forgotten to love Him, in my absorbing affection for my husband. But He is long-suffering and willing to forgive. '*Whom He loveth He chasteneth, and scourgeth every one whom He receiveth.*' I have been bitterly scourged and chastened; but once more I thank Thee, Oh my Father, that Thou hast made me to love Thee, and to praise Thee for it forever.

"I have so many kind friends who love me for my husband's sake, I am not left destitute and dependent. I have health, strength, and energy to fill the position assigned to me. I am daily fulfilling my husband's dearest wishes, doing all in my power to comfort his mother. Would that I could do more to fill his place! and his cherished projects will be carried out through my aid. His name will live, his example will guide me."

"—— HOTEL, NEW YORK, *Sept. 15th.*

"How great a change has the last year wrought in me! How much of life was crowded in its span! I have stood this day upon the spot where he first kissed me in acknowledgment of our betrothal. I sat long upon the seat to which he led me, and where he placed this ring upon my finger to link me to himself. One year ago to-day, I met him for the first time, face to face. We parted as we met, each heart filled with unacknowledged affection. Two months from that time, I was here again. *I was his wife.* Now I sit here alone and sorrowful; he is laid in his grave, and my bridal dress is exchanged for the garb of the widow."

When Mrs. Neal returned to Philadelphia, it was to begin a life of earnest and self-denying effort. Mr. Neal's property was embarked in the paper upon which he was engaged. This investment his wife preferred to retain, and she became one of the editors of the paper. Before this she had written editorials under her husband's eye; now she was to act alone. Certain departments were assigned to her, and one she almost created in its freshened beauty and value. The juvenile department, called "The Bird's Nest," had many sweet voices issuing from it besides that of "Cousin Alice," as Mrs. Neal called herself when writing for children.

Some of the best female writers of the day contributed to the paper. Many of them had begun to do so before the death of Mr. Neal; others were interested in the efforts made by the young widow to sustain the reputation of the Gazette in all points where she could, and they gladly gave her all the aid in their power. Fanny Forrester was no longer in this country, having been married the year before "Alice Lee" became Alice Neal; but "Grace Greenwood," who was then making her fame, "Edith May,"

"Estelle," Mrs. Eames, Caroline May, of New York, the Tuthills, mother and daughters, of Princeton, and others, some of whom have ended their career in the literary world, and some departed this life for a better, were the friends and co-laborers of Mrs. Neal. Their friendship encouraged her in many an hour of despondency, and when she felt the burden beyond her strength, their aid was given lovingly and generously.

In "The Bird's Nest," several young writers first dared to let the world hear of them; and some who are now full fledged, were then encouraged and borne up by the unaffected interest of Alice Neal. She became the personal friend of many a timid young debutante, who little dreamed that the warm sympathy she received came from one who was little in advance of her in age.

There was an unusual maturity in what Mrs. Neal wrote at this time, both in her prose and verse. A poem called "The Blind," was commended, for its uncommon dramatic power, by some of the best critics of verse; and if "poets learn in suffering what they teach in song," it might well have had a startling force and depth. Her youth was almost lost sight of in her position; but this did not expose her literary efforts to unkindly judgment, and her successes were numerous and gratifying.

During all the excitement of this career, on which she had entered with her whole energy, and which was at once so brilliant and so trying to one of her nature and age, Alice never lost sight of her noblest ambition. There was nothing so fascinated her as the brilliant social life that wooed her with its enticements, but there was nothing satisfying to her in this, and no praise yet touched in her the spring which could overflow her soul with peace. During the autumn she writes in her journal:

"I am strongly acted upon by external influences, moved by the emotions of those with whom I converse, by word or in books. I have been reading this morning the life of Elizabeth Fry, a great and good woman. There comes to me again the feeling which has haunted me from my earliest childhood, that I am being moulded for some noble and holy mission; that I have passed through the sea of sorrow and suffering, that my feet may be more firm upon the dry land.

"God has been leading me from the moment of my

birth; He has given me talents and placed me in a position for their rapid and judicious cultivation. I passed years burdened with ill health, and in uncongenial surroundings. 'The blind has' again 'received sight,' and health is added to all other blessings. I yearned to be loved, and He gave me the affection of a noble and generous heart, the unreserved teaching and confidence of one whose nature was unselfish and pure—wise as the serpent, harmless as the dove. I wished for literary distinction, and even now, while I am scarce a woman, my name is beginning to be heard.

"He has kindly shown me the emptiness of this world's praise, its treachery, and its deceitfulness. He removed from me my husband, yet softened the chastisement with so much mercy, that murmurs died upon my lips, and were turned to praise for His infinite goodness. He was a father to the fatherless. He has been my support and trust in my early and lonely widowhood.

"I have felt very humble and grateful this morning in recounting all this, and it has seemed to me that I could yield my whole being into His hands to be moulded by Him. I have tried to pray in truth, that He would receive me as a servant to do His pleasure. Yet I know that much of this emotion is simply the enthusiasm of my nature, and that soon, perhaps to-morrow, I shall again be yielding to pleasure and ambition. I dare not make a resolution, I have so often broken the most solemn; but I do pray most humbly that He will assist me in my struggle to learn and to perform my duty.

"I know that I am surrounded by temptations on all sides; my youth, my position, and my ambition for a brilliant life, will be constantly leading me away. I do not strive sufficiently to learn the right, or to fix and confirm the basis of my Christian belief. I do not feel that emotion which others describe as love to God and my Saviour. I am too selfish in my life and in my prayers. These are confined to my own welfare and that of my dearest friends. I do not feel, with the intensity which the subject demands, the situation of those who are without Christ, and the hope of life eternal.

"I am wavering in my resolutions to do right, and am too easily led by others. I am vain—vain of personal attractions and mental endowments. I am given to exaggeration, and have not a sufficient perception of the beauty and holiness of truth. My vanity not only fills my mind with trifling thoughts, but gives me a love of display and of universal admiration. For a time at least let my diary be a beacon, by a weekly record of my shortcomings in my attempts to serve my Heavenly Father. In His strength, and not in my own, I would begin this new life."

Some weeks later there is another indication of her struggle with a fault which she had in common with most persons of a vivid imagination. Her enthusiasm aided her imagination in the coloring she would give in her conversation.

She sometimes saw things, she says, as she would *like* to see them; "and it was very difficult to look so steadfastly that the iris-hues would disappear, leaving only the white light of truth." To correct this tendency, she strove against the ardor of her nature, encouraging any thing that dampened it—welcoming rebuffs even, and refraining from murmuring when humiliations came, as come they do to all who are prominent in society, and especially before the public eye. Her demerits were never long out of her mind; and the reviews she constantly makes of her conduct, and of her motives, could not fail to give her a wholesome self-knowledge, by which she laid the foundation for the superstructure of character which made her later years eminent. She says, under date of Oct. 10th:

"No record last week. It had, as usual, much to be repented of, and I gained very little, only I hope I am getting a greater regard for truth, for my conscience checks me, even at the shadow of its opposite. Still I *romance* a great deal.

"Let it be my care, if ever I have children to train, that they are not led into deceit through fear, as I was at one period of my life; and may I never let them know that I think the thing possible. Little liar! How often do we hear the expression without reflecting on its consequences."

Afterwards she writes:

"The sermon this morning was upon 'the love of God.' That is what I do not feel.

"'R.,' said I, as we came home from church, 'can you understand the meaning of love to God?'

"'I can,' he said.

"'Well, do you think you love God?'

"'I do,' was his earnest reply.

"Now, what *can* be the emotion? I am thankful to my Father in heaven for His daily mercies. I try to yield my will to His. I ask, when I pray, that He will make me love Him, and do all my duty by Him. But there is something to which I cannot attain. It has been the enigma of my life; and when I once feel a devoted love to God, and to His Son Jesus Christ, then I shall cease to doubt that I am His child."

This record is followed, as are many others through all her later journals, by a written prayer. In this instance the petition is for humility, patience, content, wisdom, and perfect sincerity. The simplicity, earnestness, and directness of these forms, which, she says, she found of great service, and used from time to time, though she generally uttered a spontaneous and extemporaneous prayer, are very marked. She was certainly learning to pray in the way in which she many years after directed a servant. She said then:

"Those who desire to pray acceptably, sometimes feel very unhappy because their prayers are not long enough. We must make it familiar to us, for without the help of God we are every hour in danger. Those who desire much, pray for much: those who are years uttering the petition, '*that which I see not, teach thou me*,' see their need of many things which are still hidden from you. See that your prayers are sincere, rather than lengthy, and as frequent as may be. Some force you must use toward natural inclination, for that is not to pray at all; and blessed will you be when you have learned to be much in prayer."

This was her course from the time she began in the darkness in which she now found herself, to feel her way to the Light. That she stumbled much was not strange; that sometimes the thick darkness appalled and discouraged her, was not to be wondered at; that the inconsistencies of her inner and outer life humiliated her continually, was only to be expected.

On December 12th, her wedding-day anniversary, she writes:

"The dreaded 'first year!' how often we thoughtlessly used the expression, ends to-day. This was the anniversary that was to have been a joy to us both, that was to have been kept '*with feasting and gladness.*' The first year of marriage would be passed: we should have had time to study each other's character, to appreciate worth, to correct deficiencies. After this we were to be happy forevermore—no clouds in our domestic horizon, no discords in our harmony. One year ago I became a wife—still a child in years and knowledge.

"I think a vague presentiment of evil haunted me from our first meeting. I see it as I read over our letters. I recall my emotions when married scarcely two months. I wrote in this volume a prophecy of the struggle I am now undergoing. Little did we think, as I read it over to him, how terrible the reality would be. 'You are a good child, Alice,' he said. I have just read a precious letter, in which he wrote, 'death alone part thee and me.' The parting came too soon. God only knows why we were deprived of the happiness looked forward to by us both. If it is that my life should be dedicated to His service, I pray to be content, and for strength to bear the trials I *am*, and constantly shall be, subjected to."

These trials were sharp indeed; the record of them shows how thorny her life had become as soon as she stood alone, unguided and unguarded. It might well awaken questions of the purpose God had in view in leading her through these rough ways. To those who knew her in her later years, it was made plain; to her it was mysterious, except as she saw in it the loosening of her hold on the world.

## CHAPTER VII.

### *HER STRUGGLE.*

SHE so often alludes to the struggle she was going through, that it may be as well to define it a little more clearly. She was very young for the place she held before the world, very inexperienced, and considered very charming. Her personal attractions and her conversational ability have already been described: the interest of these was heightened by the romance of the events which had given her her position. There was a rare maturity about her, the result of uncommon ability and insight; but her temptations, so fully set forth in her own language, brought snares to her path, which only more than mortal foresight and prudence could render harmless.

A gentleman who was one of Mr. Neal's partners, and who was engaged with her in the settlement of her husband's affairs, an astute man of the world, said afterwards in speaking of their connection:

> "Alice Neal was the most remarkable woman I ever met. Young girl as she was at that time, she comprehended the business details laid before her, and showed a judgment in regard to them which no other woman I ever knew could have shown—I might almost say at any age. She was a match for that proverbially close-dealing man, 'a Philadelphia lawyer.' She would have made an admirable lawyer herself."

Notwithstanding the impression made by her clear, strong mind, it was inevitable that youth and inexperience should make some grievous mistakes; but taking counsel in all things of her husband's mother, and regarding as paramount to every thing her husband's interests and reputation, she was able to show much wisdom and judgment in the administration of his affairs. Upon her fair young shoulders came the burden which had fallen from his. Her friends looked on in astonishment that she did not sink beneath it. In her need she rallied all the strength she was conscious of possessing; and those who looked to see her faint and fail beneath accumulated difficulties, saw instead the resolute opposition to every encroachment of despair, the steadfast determination, based in her simple reliance upon the source of all strength and courage, "*to endure unto the end*," and accomplish the work that was given her to do.

No words could do more justice to the principles which were now so plainly operating on her daily life, than those which we quote from an article written by one who knew her as inmately as a person can be known, reviewing the course of a life so beneficent in its results.

"Few even of those who knew her intimately, comprehended the trials and struggles, the privations and temptations which she met and overcame. The natural tendency of her temperament was ease-loving and self-indulgent. She had a keen enjoyment of all beautiful and luxurious things, a taste for social pleasures, and a perfectly natural consciousness of the admiration which her beauty and vivacity never failed to elicit. Yet with all this, to tempt her away from the path of self-denial and sacrifice which she had chosen, the instances in which she swerved from it are few and far between; while the records of her self-forgetting labors for others come in troops. That one and another might be supplied with needed comforts, she denied herself every thing but the simplest necessaries, and much that would have been considered indispensable by a majority of judges. Her dress, her table, the furnishing of her house, every personal surrounding, evinced the same principle of economy in opposition to natural tastes; but in spite of the rigid simplicity enforced, there was about all an air of grace and refinement, which was perfectly inseparable from her, and with which every thing she touched was at once invested.

"This subtle attribute was one of her chief charms: those who knew her sufficiently to appreciate the delicate shades of her character, will recognize it readily, and remember how all-pervading it was."

There are many who will recall with pleasure the rooms in their house in Seventh street, where assembled from time to time her husband's friends and her own, and her admirers, for some there were whose professions of admiration had little of friendship in them, as we shall see.

In the drawing-room, at the window farthest from the entrance, was seated Mr. Neal's mother; after a certain hour in the morning that high-backed, morocco-covered easy chair was rarely vacant. Beside her on the deep window seat, and about her on chairs and small tables, were the latest papers and reviews, American and foreign, giving this remarkable old lady intelligence of a world in which her interest was as fresh as it had been fifty years before. The Italian clock on the table kept no better time than Mrs. Neal in her daily routine, nor to the casual visitor seemed more mechanical. But a quick eye and a fine sense of propriety lay beneath this calm demeanor, and nothing that occurred was lost upon her, as Alice flitted about, or her visitors came in and went out.

There were pictures on the walls, books and pictures on the tables, an open piano, a shaded lamp—everywhere articles of *virtu*, in keeping with the tastes and pursuits of the two ladies, and the marked individual air which their surroundings always possessed.

Opening from this large room was a smaller one—the attractive library and study, with its rows of choice books on the shelves, occupying one side of the room, the etagère also filled with books, but crowned by a tiny work basket, showing that the habitual occupant of the room was a woman, and a disposition of easy chairs and hassocks, which was always inviting. The papers on the table beside the open desk were always in the nicest order; the weights and clasps everywhere about the room held no ill-assorted and carelessly-arranged treasures; every thing was exquisitely neat and truly feminine. A few pictures and ornaments were gracefully disposed about the apartment, a vase of flowers usually found place on some table or stand; but the room took its character from its book shelves, and its occupant, who sat writing generally on a little footstool, her portfolio in her lap, and her Bible on the chair beside her, indicating to a close observer what always preceded her morning's work.

Miss Leslie, whose fame was of years' standing, was a very sincere friend of the young writer, giving her always the advantage of her experience and shrewd observation. It was an event in Alice's life when she made the acquaintance of the author of "The Atlantic Tales," which had been one of the favorite books of her childhood. A clear-sighted and society-trained old lady as she was, Miss Leslie, with her keen insight and her wise counsels, was a friend with whom intercourse never lost its zest for Alice. Years of life abroad, association with eminent literary persons and artists in England and in this country, the artistic training which Charles Leslie's sister would be likely to have, the philosophical development which was the natural tendency of her mind, and which the sister-in-law of Henry Carey had opportunity to cultivate, combined with her native shrewdness to make Miss Leslie's friendship an untold advantage to one who was finding material for her work in the same channels, though using it so differently. Mr. Carey, of whom we have spoken, was very kind to the young aspirant; Dr. John Hart, a fine scholar and good critic, admired and praised her; Mrs. Peters, the accomplished wife of the British Consul, a lady of taste, culture, literary association, and social preëminence, served her with friendship and warm interest; indeed all were her friends, in the literary circles of the city, who were capable of appreciative and disinterested friendship.

But there was a shaded side to this fair picture. That Alice Neal was young and admired, was enough to make the malignant and envious critical. Her success was bitter to some—the admiration she excited in society, to others. There were plenty who would flatter her, and malign her with equal fervor, and she had, in her inexperience, no test by which to try them. There were some who were older adepts in social life, who appealed to her love of pleasure, and lured her by temptations to frivolity, that they might gratify their own contemptible baseness of nature, which would have looked coolly, if not complacently, on the havoc they might have made with her happiness or reputation.

She frequently visited New York, where her only brother now resided, and became acquainted while there with Miss Lynch, Ann S. Stephens, Mrs. Seba Smith, and others belonging to the literary cliques which these writers represented. Such associations with those to whom, as a school-girl, she had looked up with the deference their genius inspired, was perfectly delightful to her. The excitement of these visits was great, and to her youth, and the self-enforced severity of her life, not always wholesome.

In one of these visits she overheard, at a social

party, a remark which opened her eyes to the baseness from which a love of gossip springs, and to which it leads. Her own name was used in a manner which startled and wounded her. In the strength of the pain she suffered, she at once resolved to court an investigation, which should enable her to define her position, secure her standing, and sustain herself. The record of her conversations with those whom she had considered her friends, is most pathetic, when we remember that a young, warm-hearted woman, almost a child still, had thus to take up her own cause. She traced the falsehoods to their sources; in some cases it was to remarks made about her by those in whose protestations of friendship she had trusted, and to whom she had yielded her confidence. In a conversation of some hours with such a person, who finally dropped the veil and allowed herself to be seen in her true colors, Alice learned unsuspected lessons of life, and the vanity of social distinctions and professions. She saw how treacherous had been the quicksands which, in her ignorance, she had mistaken for the solid land, and how narrow her escape, which she regarded with unfeigned thankfulness. This most prominent failure was not the only one she had to face; and she might have been sick at heart, with all her philosophy and courage, if some had not borne the ordeal and proved themselves true and noble. But it would seem from the record, though Alice herself left the impression unwillingly or unconsciously, that some of these even had been wanting in the moral courage, which is one of the most prominent elements of a worthy friendship.

It is a matter of wonder to all true-hearted people, how a friend can see another, whom she might influence and guide, to whom her wisdom and experience would be untold treasures, drifting on the rocks that lie unsuspected beneath the smiling sunshine, and in the summer seas. If the whole story of this period of trial could be given in the simple and touching words in which Alice has recorded it—"for a beacon," she says, "to myself"—it would be a potent rebuke to the selfish and cold-hearted, no less than to the false and malignant. The world is full of those whose calm natures and narrow souls are never tempted over the line of propriety, and whose sharp eyes are ready to detect the first footstep beyond it, while their souls are filled with a virtuous indignation, "which points the moral and adorns the tale," with which they are so ready. They forget the new commandments our Saviour gave, and remember only the severity of the law which has appalled them into virtuous lives. Loyalty, tenderness, and charity are as unknown to them as the propensities which they criticize with so much zest.

And, besides these virtuous souls, are the inefficient who shrink from the exertion, the cautious who will not interfere, or are afraid to commit themselves by counsel; and those of still colder natures, who watch with curious eyes the mental and moral processes they do not care to interrupt. Alice, earnest, ardent, courageous, and demonstrative, was a fine subject for such critical review and examination.

She shrunk from no test, however painful, in the search for truth upon which she had entered. It cost her her trust in some whom, in her ignorance of their nature, she had counted friends. It cost her an agony of anxious effort and suspense, and an amount of courage which proved the sincerity of her purpose. It cost her humiliation and heart-sinking, but it brought her treasures, wisdom that one can only learn after such expenditure; a knowledge of human nature, which is only acquired by such opportunities; a power of self-restraint, which brought back some of the reserve of her younger years; and some friends, whom she could henceforth trust through all her life, however varied its course.

She saw how she had been misled by the *ignis fatuus* of worldly friendships, how she had mistaken flattery for appreciation, professions for worth and honor; she saw herself misrepresented and blamed where she knew her motives had been pure and worthy, for her very good was evil-spoken of, and a weaker nature would have succumbed to the fierceness of the attack. *But to her this was a seed-sowing from which the world reaped a harvest of sweet counsel, and a wisdom divine in its charity.* Well might she say of herself, that she passed through deep waters, that her feet might be firm upon the dry land.

"Never," she writes, "was the goodness of God more manifest in all the dealings which my life shows. It was *very hard;* no one can ever know what I suffered. I saw how a careless word or action had sufficed for a foundation for their ill report; how often, in the simple consciousness of my integrity, I had been rash, and had so appeared defiant in action; how my vanity had sometimes betrayed me; and my very freedom from the faults I encountered in others, had made me as unguarded as I was unsuspicious. Conventionalities often originate in narrowness and pettiness, but they are respectable as safeguards. I have learned to hold these at their true value in losing much simple faith. I understand, however, these lines in 'The Lost Bower':

'Some respect to social fictions
Hath been also lost by me;
And some generous genuflexions,
Which my spirit offered free,
To the pleasant old conventions of our false Humanity.'"

In her journal, under date of July 9th, 1848, she writes:

"As this is the Sunday preceding the solemn anniversary of my husband's death, and, as I solemnly trust, of my spiritual birth, I have resolved to commence a review of my first year of widowhood, knowing no fitter preparation for that sad day of fasting and of prayer. I know the record will convict me of much that will be bitter in recollection, as well as wrong in commission.

"First, with regard to my spiritual progress: let me look back and trace from the hour of my renewed dedication to God, all that has had any influence on my profession as a Christian.

"At first there was a constant struggle with fearful recollections of the past, anxieties for the future, and present suffering. I depended too little on the grace of God, too much on my individual strength."

Then with a review of some of the trials which have been recorded, she says:

"And so I prayed for true friends, and in answer to my prayer I found Mrs. T. and her daughters, who have been my best help in my religious life, who have counselled, warned, and comforted me. Mrs. M. has done battle for me with some disposed to be malignant, and Mr. and Mrs. P. have told me of my faults and given me a sister's care.

"Early in the spring I paid brother a visit. Once more I grew heedless and thoughtless. It was in Lent when I had solemn thoughts with regard to my duty of joining the visible Church of Christ. I could not feel that I was a Christian, although I was trying to act rightly; but I tried feebly, and I could not resolve to give up the pomp and vanity of the world.

"At the commencement of Lent, my friend C. T. passed a morning in my study. She spoke to me of my many temptations, and asked my conscience if I would not be safer in the church. I had no acquaintance with my rector, and no acquaintances with the exception of my friend's family, who could at all encourage me in 'well doing.' I listened in silence, but resolved the next day to discover myself to Mr. Odenheimer, the Rector of St. Peter's, where I had attended church since Joseph's death.

"On that day, after the homily had been read, I lingered in the pew, while a sense of suffocation came over me. I saw an acquaintance cross the church, and speak to Mr. Odenheimer; with sudden resolution I joined them. Our rector smiled pleasantly as I approached, and seemed surprised when he found that Mrs. Neal was before him.

"I told him all. I poured out my doubts and my wishes. He listened kindly and attentively; he 'did not wish me to enter the Episcopal Church, unless I was fully decided in all points of its faith,' and he encouraged me to go on in 'well doing.' The worst effect of the morning's conversation was that my vanity was stimulated. I began to think that I *was* doing well, and it made me resolve to pray against *vain glory*.

"In the winter, when first praying to know my work in the vineyard, an opportunity offered for me to take a Bible class in a Moyamensing Mission School. The girls were from a lower class in society, profoundly ignorant, and I should even have said uninteresting. Gradually I came to love them, and to look forward to meeting them weekly with pleasure. I have them still under my charge, but I sometimes fear that I am a blind leader of the blind.

For those I pray that I may be able to watch for their souls, as one who must give account. God grant that it be not a fearful rendering."

And here comes the sharp introspection which followed a second visit to New York that year, the memorable visit which has been spoken of. In finishing her account of the ordeal she passed through, she says:

"I consider that God is answering my prayer for humility, *but in a way that I had not expected.*

"On the whole, I trace a little improvement; I humbly acknowledge my backslidings, with much neglect of duty; and I confess that wherein I have attained, it has been in the Divine strength."

She records a visit paid by Mr. Neal's mother, his cousin, and herself, to her husband's grave at Laurel Hill, and says:

"So ends the anniversary of Joseph's death. The first milestone of my life is left behind. I am thankful for the pause beside it, for the struggle of the year, and for the calm which it has brought. May this coming year have a better record.

"Lead me not into temptation,
But deliver me from evil."

## CHAPTER VIII.

*THE TENOR OF HER LIFE IN PHILADELPHIA.*

IN the autumn of 1848 Alice Neal again visited New York. She speaks of meeting many of the literary people with whom she had had so much agreeable intercourse in the spring. But she was becoming disenchanted, learning to distinguish true from false friends, and to estimate rightly the meretricious brilliancy of much of the social life which had been so fascinating to her, when it terminated the vista into which her girlhood had looked.

Some of the friends made during this year were friends for lifetime; they were those whose Christian principles made them not "of the world" in which they moved. There was already visible in Alice the ennobling influence of her new life; and she now began to interest and attract those who recognized her earnestness, and her serious idea of life, about which were twining the graces of a religious character. One dear friend, whose letters she kept very choicely, and whose gift of a "Bogatsky" she gratefully acknowledges, was of service to her in many ways; her very life of devotedness, of the sublimest self-sacrifice, of cheerfulness under the sharpest trials, and courage when the unaided human spirit would inevitably have given way, and trailed its pinions in the dust; all this was to Alice's sympathizing and appreciative nature a lesson of might, and strengthening, reminding her that she, too, "might make her life sublime." She often said, when speaking with those who knew the recesses of this strong, rich inner life, that she could not fitly express her acknowledgment to that friend who so unconsciously taught and so nobly enforced her lessons.

In the latter part of the year, learning that some near and beloved friends and relations were going to California, then a new world, where life was beset with perils, she went over to New

York to give them "bon voyage," and up to Hudson in a violent snow storm, because she thought she might be some comfort to those left alone by this departure. It was her peculiarity, that though very sensitive to weather-changes, and feeling intensely and pervadingly the influence of the sullen or the stormy east wind, or the despondency brought by the warm south-west, she was never deterred by fierce wind, or driving storm, from the accomplishment of any purpose which she might have in her mind. Indeed, when the violence of the weather amounted to an obstacle, it was sure to rouse in her those qualities with which she was always ready to confront "the lion in her path."

The principle of *duty* was coming now to be the spur of her life, and it made her indomitable. The records of the resolute manner in which she henceforth performed all duties, especially those toward the sorrowing and comfortless, would fill this volume, if such a record had been kept. But little is known of this, except such instances as abide in the hearts of those she served, or in the memories of those to whom accident revealed the secrets of a life "spent in bearing the burdens of others." Her journal has rarely even a casual mention of such service. As an intimate friend said of her years after—" the right hand could not know what the left was doing," so delicately and privately were her self-denials, sacrifices, and charities performed.

It was while she was in New York, at this time, that she made the acquaintance of Mr. Haven, in whom she became interested, at first, from the circumstance that he also was just leaving for California. He was at once one of her admirers; but this was not noticeable, for these seemed to spring up in troops wherever she alighted. But before he sailed, the acquaintance had taken a warmer character, and she had been induced to partially respond to his feeling, and to give him a promise to correspond with him while he should remain in California. He was not a religious man, and her gift to him at parting of a well-marked Bible, was very characteristic.

The engagement into which they entered was so partial, and so entirely private, that she returned to Philadelphia, and her life went on as before, this interest sending no visible ripple over its surface.

Soon after this, Read the artist was engaged to illustrate a volume of "Female Prose Writers," which Professor Hart was to edit. A crayon drawing was made of Alice, which was engraved in London, and which, with others, adorns that volume. It is an idealized picture, but to those who saw the spiritual lineaments, the most satisfactory picture that is left of her.

In speaking of her in this volume, Professor Hart says, in reference to her life with her husband's mother:

"To this excellent woman, now seventy-two years of age, with a filial love like that of Ruth to Naomi, she has said, '*I will never leave thee nor forsake thee.*' Since the death of Mr. Neal, the two ladies have continued to live together, the younger gracefully acknowledging the rich stores of experience, the varied reading, the fine tastes, and judicious counsels of her aged companion, which have more than compensated for her own more active exertions.

"Mrs. Neal is one of our youngest writers, and what is of most favorable omen, shows, in her writings, constant signs of improvement. In the language of a contemporary critic, who writes on this subject *con amore*, and whose opinion we make our own, 'Her poetry has more maturity than her prose, for the gift of song comes to the bard as to the bird, direct from heaven. Polish and metrical correctness may be added to genuine poetry, but it is doubtful whether the fount be not as pure and sparkling at its first gush, as when quietly flowing on in a deeper stream. Mrs. Neal's prose contributions are continually improving, and the knowledge which, with uncommon industry, she is constantly acquiring, will enlarge her sphere of thought and illustration; and better yet, the religious tenor of her writings shows she is guarded by principle, which will strengthen her intellect, and make her in after years an ornament and a blessing to our land.'"

The reference made by the Professor to the relation existing between Mrs. Neal and herself, is gracefully alluded to in a sonnet which she used as a dedication to the book, bearing the title of "The Gossips of Rivertown." This was in two volumes, and the second was chiefly composed of stories and poems—the only collection of the kind she ever made, though she might have filled many volumes in this way.

"The Gossips of Rivertown" is the only book she could ever wish unpublished. The feeling in which it originated has been explained in a former chapter; and years after its publication she tried to purchase the plates and suppress the work, because of the personalities in it into which she so sincerely regretted having been betrayed. It is the only record which shows what control she needed to exercise over her perception of the ludicrous, and her remarkable power of sarcasm. She was so humiliated, however, as she became conscious of the indulgence in which she had allowed herself, that she had no satisfaction in the very decided "cleverness" she showed, and of which, as well of the other traits mentioned, there is no other striking evidence. She always spoke of it with pain and mortification. The sonnet alluded to should not be lost, however:

"As Ruth of old wrought in her kinsman's field,
From the uneven stubble, patiently
Gathering the corn, full hands had lavished free,
Nor paused from wind or sun her brow to shield—
So have I gleaned where others boldly reap;
Their sickles flashing in the ripened grain,
Their voices swelling in the harvest strain,
Go on before me up the toilsome steep.
And thus I bind my sheaf at eventide,
For thee, my more than mother; and I come
Bearing my burden to the quiet home,
Where thou didst welcome me, a timid bride;
Where now thy blessed presence, day by day,
Cheereth me onward in a lonely way."

The time was coming when Alice had resolved to disclose to the world her religious standpoint; and we find the following entry in her journal:

"*Feb. 4th*, 1849.

"A bright and beautiful Sabbath, yet I indulged in indolence; and as I was preparing for church in a gust of passion, ———, as usual, the provocation" (alluding to a person in the family who was a great trial to her), "my mind would wander in prayer. It is the third Sunday before Lent; at the close of that solemn fast, I hope to be a member of the Church of God. Let me remind myself of the necessity for increased watchfulness, lest by any means I be drawn again into the world I have so nearly renounced. Let me prepare for extraordinary temptations.

"I had some of my Sunday-school class present this morning. I hope I am thankful for this, the more that they seemed interested in the subject of the lesson, which was prayer. Through a remark of one of the girls, I saw more plainly than ever, the evil of letting the thoughts wander in prayer. I proposed to her as I have to myself, the habit of praying aloud, from which I have always shrunk. I tried to pray for them on my return home, as well as for S. and T. and my brother. Let me choose these, with my class, as subjects of earnest and special prayer for the year."

"*5th Feb.*

"Ill, but worked on; a visitor came in, and I was not

as careful as I must be; I must not trifle, even by a look. If ever I overcome this great fault of my life, I shall feel as if a victory was won."

"*7th Feb.*

"Visitors all the morning—Mrs. Hale, Judge K., 'Kate Campbell,' Mrs. K., C. M. Then a music lesson. I have tried to *think* in all this whirl; I have so many interruptions."

"*11th Feb.*

"I had an excellent class. I feel encouraged. Oh that I may do my whole duty to these dear girls! I do think my mind wanders less in prayer, and that I am able to pray more earnestly. Let me remember to *watch* as well as pray."

She then goes on to speak of the impression produced upon her mind, when coming from church, by meeting group after group, some of them evidently "taking sweet counsel together, as they came from the House of God in company," while she walked on solitary and lonely. She certainly found little encouragement amongst her habitual associates, to lead the elevated spiritual life to which she aspired, and which alone seemed to promise her satisfaction and peace.

She had another source of discomfort now—it was in remembering her promise to Mr. Haven, and the anticipation that the consummation of her engagement, whenever it might come, would oblige her to leave Mrs. Neal. She tries to allay the feeling of disturbance, by reminding herself that it is too far in the future for her to suffer real distress, as she could not fail to do, if she expected soon to leave her to whom all the remembrance of her husband, "her best friend," as she never failed to consider him, bound her. Years at least were before her, during which she might remain with the desolate mother. To comfort and brighten that lonely life, she was willing, while her strength held out, to encounter toil and privation, if necessary. There were many satisfactions in her life; there was pleasure in the appreciation she received, in the honest friends she culled from the many proffering friendship, in the aid she could afford to young writers, and in the substantial assistance she was able, through the increasing remuneration her pen brought her, to extend to those who were in need. She had not yet grown weary in her routine of life; but if the prospect of another sometimes flashed over her mind, where she would be guarded by a sheltering love, is it wonderful that, storm-beaten as she had been, and as she might be again, she should begin to dream of refuge and rest?

In addition to the stories, editorials, and poems that came constantly from her tireless pen, she wrote "Helen Morton's Trial," a story of a child's temporary blindness, which could not but be touchingly graphic, when she knew so well "that of which she affirmed." At the suggestion of her rector, she submitted it for approval to Bishop Henshaw, of Rhode Island. The Bishop wrote very kindly and approvingly about it, for which she was most grateful. This was the first of a series of books suitable for Sunday-school use, containing the history of Helen Morton, and, with its companions, was destined to great popularity, not only in the Episcopal families which it reached through their publication society, but wherever pure and earnest religious teaching for children was valued. Among her papers was found a letter from a stranger, evidently a lady of culture as well as of piety, asking that a fourth volume should be added to the series, carrying Helen's life, with its lessons, still further.

She planned also a volume of religious poetry,

collected from different sources, which she called "Sabbath Chimes;" but some untowardness prevented its publication. She also planned, to be executed by herself, a series of poems, to be entitled "Thoughts in Lent."

These holy days of the church were always of peculiar interest to her. The spirit of this institution especially appealed to her. She prized all the associations, all "the means of grace" which each season brought. There was only delight and comfort in the opportunities afforded her for church-going, for freedom from secular cares; and through all her life we find her giving herself for this Lent or that, special subjects to be remembered constantly in supplication.

"*March 25th.*

"One week from this morning is our Confirmation. I do earnestly pray that I may be in a proper spirit to receive the rite. I am so near the Zoar of the Church, God keep me from looking back, and afterwards give me strength '*to escape to the mountains.*' The past week I have endeavored to set a watch upon the door of my lips, but have continually forgotten my aim. This shall be renewed for the week to come."

Having made up her mind to become a communicant at St. Peter's, she thought it her duty to work in its Sabbath-school, which would make it necessary to give up her class in the mission school. This was a painful thing to do, as she had grown to be much interested in her pupils. She informed the clergyman, who had charge of the mission, of her intention, and in a long conversation acquainted him with the circumstances and state of mind of each scholar.

Now comes a record of the day of her confirmation, and the Bishop's address written down with her usual accurate memory of all she heard. She had not intended to partake of the communion till Easter, but she felt constrained to do so on this day.

The parting with her class was painful to all —the scholars weeping bitterly; nor could she restrain her own tears.

She recounts with much gratitude, that there was no opposition made in the family to the step she was taking, but that she was treated with uncommon kindness and consideration by them.

"*May 6th.*

"My first Sunday as teacher at St. Peter's. I have a

very interesting class, and like it better than the mission school. I sat with my little people in church; they behaved well, and we are on the best of terms. I do believe I was intended 'to feed the Lambs.' God grant that I administer no poison with the 'sincere milk of the Word.'"

## CHAPTER IX.

*HER LIFE IN PHILADELPHIA.*

LIFE was taking on sterner aspects for Alice Neal with every new year. One by one the delusions with which she had begun it were fading into "the light of common day." Where she had found one worthy friend, she had proved two false, envious women and men whose disinterestedness was only on the lip, if even its pretence was found about them. Their never large income grew smaller, and Alice toiled all the more indefatigably, and sought at every avenue a chance of success.

L. A. Godey, Esq., of the "Lady's Book," "a gentleman amongst publishers," as a cynical writer once called him, when speaking of the difficulty writers often found in getting paid for their contributions to our periodical literature, had been a friend of Mr. Neal and his interest in the young widow was always of the sincerest and noblest sort. Seeing her efforts, he gave her the encouragement of an offer for regular contributions to the pages of his magazine, and placed an editorial department under her control. Besides this engagement, she sent off stories and poems in every direction, working on her own paper meanwhile with the greatest assiduity. She increased the economy which already marked her personal expenditure, while the comforts of the house remained unabated, and the number of those who were more or less her pensioners increased rather than diminished.

Her suffering from attacks of headache became greater; her strength was less, and the attacks more numerous and prostrating; no great excitement or fatigue could pass without this penalty being incurred. She resisted the enervating tendency of such suffering with positive heroism—passing few days where work was not the rule, rest the exception.

Her spiritual life was characterized by discouragements arising from a sharp sense of her failures in her efforts to overcome faults, and by renewed energy in her endeavors. A friend, one of the very few who were admitted to the penetralia of her soul, writes of her in reference to her course at this time:

"With her sweet playfulness, her outspoken variable feeling, her quick perception alike of the ludicrous, the noble, and the good, her character was most fitted to encourage those who, struggling with the impulsiveness and excitability almost inseparable from delicacy of health and organization, often feel as if, in their very temperament (to those who misunderstand it), there is apparent inconsistency with their deep and serious spiritual perceptions and aims."

That she never gave up effort, under the influence of any discouragement, temporal or spiritual, was her distinguishing trait, and the secret of her final success. That the rebound was always in proportion to the depression, showed the elastic power of her mind and the firmness of her underlying principle. She more and more excluded pleasures from her life, and bent to her toil. She writes years afterwards:

"I cannot trust myself to speak of the racking, dizzy headaches which would follow a restless night of wild plans *to get money*, money, not for myself—my wants grew less all the time, with the narrowing of my personal ambition—but for those whom I found I could aid, for the comfort of those I loved, as I was finding out, better than myself, for those whom God's providence was bringing into the line of my life. In a great measure, I tried to write first and find a market afterwards. I had three bitter and cruel (then cruel) disappointments before Mr. Appleton began to publish for me, or Mr. Godey had made my contributions monthly. You do not know, no one can ever know, the pecuniary struggle, close and sharp, of those two years. I stinted myself in every thing. Once to those who might, I thought, have shared one burden with me, my self-righteousness disclosed itself in a letter, which I have been ashamed of ever since.

"From that moment I left off saying, 'Lord, what shall this man do?' I said instead, '*Lord, I thank thee that thus far I have been able to do. Do not punish me by leaving me to sit idle and see any want.* If I ought to have help in the work I have undertaken, put it into the hearts of others, and provide them the way; if not, let me rest content that it is my duty, not theirs.' I have prayed that others might be spared trials in life. As He put the desire and prayer into my mind, so He has placed the power into my hands to avert these trials in some cases. He has in many ways prospered me abundantly, and has granted me so many of my prayers, that I have learned to put away care for the future, and live almost entirely in the present; and then I have such a blessed trust for what time I am afraid as I remember the past, that now I am not conscious of anxiety for any thing. As some one said in a book I was reading recently, 'In looking back, even I do not see where the struggle has been.' "

At this same time, writing to a person who was seeking a publisher in vain, she says:

"I think I see the wisdom of the returned story. Success would have tempted you beyond your strength; besides, what time and strength you do have, God may have consecrated '*to a vessel of honor*,' and He would not suffer you to waste on trifling stories what He calls for in His especial service. I feel this about you. I have done so ever since you took up your pen in earnest. I have always felt, when I was met so distinctly by a rebuff, that there was an angel in the way, though I could not see it there, and I ceased to beat the poor beast that refused to carry me—I mean of late, since I began to think how every moment and hour could be best economized.

"Your troubles are those that hurry, and worry, and unfit for mental productiveness, or exertion even. You should seek, for your health of body and mind, to lessen rather than to increase your engagements.

"Does God exact day labor,
Light denied?"

"Get your John Milton, and read the whole of that for the fiftieth time. It is the greatest possible comfort to me, though I never can believe that Miss Barrett did not write it instead of Milton."

These letters were written long years after the time in her life of which we are speaking; but they embody the wisdom which was the gain of these severe lessons—a wisdom which made her life broad and strong in its serene current, and which enriched all lives bordering on the stream of hers.

In May 17th, 1851, she makes the following entry in her journal:

"It is Sunday night—a dropping rain without, mamma and I alone, the dear parlor lighted by the solar lamp, Joseph's gift that pleasant afternoon. The books, the pictures, the open piano: let me daguerreotype the scene for years that are to come, when mamma is lying beside Joseph, and I have another home.

"There is an engraving on the table, a proof of Mr. Furness' picture of myself, which has just arrived from London. *Is all this real?* the scenes I have passed through during the last five years! And here am I, drifting out to an unknown future, holding days as dark, perhaps, as some in the past, for youth and romance will have faded, and friends of to-day will be afar off, or dead then.

"A person came here yesterday, who told me he had

seen my picture in a log-cabin out West, and that my little books '*were doing good*,' and that I was loved and praised for them. My dreams realized! But how is it with me?

"R. and Mr. M. have been in this evening, as they have been every Sunday evening for the last five years. I have been cross, and rude, and uncharitable. When I think I am doing so well, pride and self-love are always ready to get the better of my good resolutions. Yet I do think my principles are more clearly defined, my practice not always *quite* so faulty. But alas! I am still on the borders of sin, and always in the midst of temptation!

"This journal is to me a series of waymarks, by which I trace the graduations of thought and feeling which make me what I am. It is egotistical, of course; but it is meant for no eye but my own.

"I have been to church but once to-day. I have yielded completely to sloth. It is one of my great faults, so many others spring from it."

It was during this year that her engagement to Mr. Haven became known. It excited a great deal of comment, and occasioned many strictures. There were not wanting those who thought or said that it would be most cruel for her to leave Mrs. Neal; the consideration and sacrifice of so much bright life was forgotten by them, in the monstrous possibility of her finding happiness in any other course of life! Then it could not but occasion a remark that she whose tastes and principles were so marked should have bound herself to one who would have no religious sympathy with her, and no sympathy in her tastes, no appreciation possibly of the elevation of her life in its self-abnegation, and its perpetual aspiration. In a poem called "Unmasking," having for its motto, "They call me heartless when I am only strong," she refers to her early bereavement, to the burden she had borne so many years uncheered, and so often unappreciated, and then says:

"And I go forth *alone*, to brave
Life's falsehood and its scorn;
Remembering that its cold deceit
Thou, too, hast nobly borne,
And with a pure humility,
Its offered honors worn.

This thought hath made me strong to check
The bitterness of grief;
Hath nerved my heart to bear the pain
Which Time brings no relief;
*Yet I am censured that my love*
*For thee hath been so brief!*

So brief! ah well! I only ask
They may not have to bear
One half the loneliness I know,
One tithe of my despair;
Our Saviour for his enemies
Through death-pangs breathed a prayer."

Alice Neal's feeling for the husband of her youth admitted no question. To the close of her life his name was uttered with a reverential tenderness; but her loyalty to this dream of her girlhood, from which she awoke to life's realities, did not enjoin upon her the inner solitude, or the toil, or the exposure to the blast, from which nothing would shield her now but a husband's care, and love, and guidance.

It was her peculiarity, that she judged always *for herself* of any important step she might have in view. She did not form her judgments hastily, or without looking at the question on every side, and especially without praying much over it.

Having done this, all she could do, she would remain quiet, the question apparently unmooted even in her own mind. This was in advance of the formation of a judgment; she was quiet, because she was watching for what she considered

God's leading. This method of procedure kept her often from asking advice when the asking was expected, and made her sometimes appear opinionated and arrogant. It was not uncommon for her to say:

> "I have been thinking over my plans for M. I must wait for light to see which way to move. As I can do nothing but this, I will put the matter out of my mind; it would be only a waste of time to go over the same ground again, when no conclusion is possible at present."

Her sister having passed the summer of 1850 in Philadelphia, in the autumn of that year Alice accompanied her and her husband to New York, and spent a few weeks there during the sensation occasioned by the coming of Jenny Lind. She gave herself up with great freshness and sense of enjoyment to the charm of the music, and scarcely less to the interest she felt personally in the singer. An evening passed with her at her hotel was an era to Alice, though Jenny Lind singing *Casta Diva*, and Jenny Lind conversing in her deep, guttural tones, seemed beings of different mould and endowment. Her personal attraction consisted in the single-mindedness of the fair Swede, the force and purity of her character, and her unaffected charity.

The illness of her brother this year brought to Alice fresh care and anxiety, and with this came losses in business, "bringing care upon care, and sorrow upon sorrow." She occupied herself with striving in every way to accomplish her purposes. The tact which was so eminent in her, that it enhanced every attraction, and was, after all that can be said in description of her personally, the most magical of her charms, that which eluded the last analysis of her powers of fascination, was her best reliance in her business affairs. Energy, courage, and tact, were the elements of character which constrained success for her.

Exercising these unsparingly, she did not fail to reap the benefit of them. She was able to effect an arrangement with the Messrs. Appleton to publish the first volume of her very popular series, called "The Home Books." Each of these had a proverbial title, and the title of each describes the phase of life in which it was written, and out of whose experience it grew. This first book was "No such Word as Fail." How significant of the history of this year of endeavor, of disappointment, and of success!

She also wrote, during this year, a second part of Helen Morton, which she called "Watch and Pray," a title as significant of the lessons she was learning in her spiritual life.

She speaks simply, but pathetically, of the trouble she was having in regard to the Gazette; for, clever and wise as she was getting to be, she was after all only a slender little woman, hardly out of her girlhood; and her partners were astute men, themselves embarrassed by the precarious success of a literary journal. She wrote to her brother-in-law, who was engaged in the same kind of an undertaking:

> "It is very pleasant to have a literary paper of one's own; but it is a very unprofitable investment, a most expensive hobby, and no one has any business to undertake it on a smaller income than $25,000 per annum!"

She says:

> "I have such depressing struggles in view of my duty, so much doubt about the future, that I sometimes do not sleep o' nights; but a clear trust in heaven alternates with the wretchedness unspeakable—a trust as clear as the sunshine in the sky while I write, cloudless, satisfying."

6

On a scrap of paper without date, but found in this volume of her journal, she writes:

"I have often thought what a mistake it was in nature to make me so small! With all the ardor and enthusiasm pent up in my heart, with all the wild fancy and impetuous, headlong impulse, the strong will, the self-centred egotism, the power of endurance, and the strange and terrible scenes of my life, I should have had some response in my physical frame. I should have been strong, full. Yet I have no pride with which to arch a stately threat, or sweep the ground as such a woman would. It is a defect in my nature that I have no strong pride; the fire is quickly kindled, and as quickly dies. It is a strange thing that I have accomplished most in the world by an acquired virtue, by industry rather than talent."

It will be seen how indomitable this industry was, as well as how unselfish the purposes for which it was exercised. Sleep and rest were her best medicines when exhausted by fatigue or work. She always ate daintily and sparingly, but she slept as heartily as a tired child—a deep, dreamless slumber, from which she was roused with difficulty. Toward morning her sleep was soundest and most refreshing; and often, when awakened, she would plead for a little more time, and hence was almost always a late riser.

As is usual with persons of her temperament, her evenings were long and bright, prolonged often to "the small hours," when life seemed to culminate, as if the chalice were then freshly brimmed with the richest wines. No one who saw her in these choice moods will forget their rare fascinations. It was hard to recognize in the morning—wakening slowly and reluctantly, like an unrested child—the bright and sparkling being of the previous evening. Through all the morning there seemed to be a slow unfolding of the earthly cumbering, each removal bringing its own gleam of spiritual life, till the charm of the bright soul was again revealed in its beauty.

Hence she knew nothing of "fresh morning hours." Her first conscious impulse was "work," her first thought "duty."

A friend who slept lightly, to whom indeed food was all that sleep was to Alice, remonstrated with her once on her late rising.

"*I sleep to live*, as you eat," she replied. "You say you have no respect for me till mid-day. I do not think I have much for myself till some time after I awake; nor then, till my spiritual nature is fairly roused. I have often wondered if any one else was as soulless as I am, sometimes for hours; my conscience first brings me to consciousness. If it grows, and characterizes me, and I hope to come more and more under its influence, I may yet be an early riser! But I think I shall be a compact of the virtues by that time, over whom the flesh will have no sway."

Yet for years this lover of sleep, and of her ease, who could so long defend her practice of late rising, was an early riser to accomplish properly the day's duties, and to give time for constantly increasing engagements.

# CHAPTER X.

## *WINTER IN CHARLESTON.*

N the autumn of 1851 her brother-in-law, coming North, found Alice wearied and depressed by the peculiar and painful trials of that year. There had been no external flagging, but her wings were wearied with her long flight, and bruised by the buffetting with the storm of untoward circumstances which had assailed her for some time past. Again, as in the year previous, her record could have been "care upon care, sorrow upon sorrow."

Yielding to the persuasion of her brother, and in consideration of the ill health of her sister, rather than with the purpose of recruiting her own exhausted energies, much as she needed this, she returned with Mr. Richards to Charleston, in October. She did not intend to spend the winter there; but month after month went by, and it was late in February before she left a city whose hospitalities had been so abundant and so grateful to her.

Her enjoyment, never lacking zest while she had any strength, was very keen during this visit. Her name was well known, her little books were exceedingly popular, the story of her life was interesting, and "Mrs. Neal" was admired and courted wherever she appeared.

Never was she personally more attractive than at this period. Her slight figure was always tastefully and gracefully arrayed, although with a girlish simplicity. No persuasion could induce her to wear ornaments in her hair, unless occasionally a natural flower, worn with the careless ease of a child.

"Mrs. Neal is here," said a lady one evening to a guest.

"Yes," replied the gentleman; "I was told she was in the room, and have occupied myself trying to find her."

"Oh, you would never know her from any

preconceived idea. She is in that group by the piano; they are begging her to sing."

"You don't mean that that young girl in white is Mrs. Neal, the writer? I thought that was some bright young creature, just from school, fluttering her wings in society for the first time, though her ease of manner puzzled me. Such pretty little hands and girlish arms, and masses of brown hair put up so simply; such a fresh bloom, and so unhackneyed in manner generally, I never would have believed it!"

She was very fond of riding, and, for health's sake, at the recommendation of her physician, she had been for some time the pupil, in Philadelphia, of a celebrated riding-master. The fine weather of a Southern winter made the exercise charming. A gentleman well known in the literary world as one of the most industrious and prolific writers in our country, called while she was out riding one afternoon, and sat awaiting her return.

She came in attired in her well-fitting dark green habit, the "Jenny Lind" hat, then in vogue, surmounting the heavy braids which set off her youthful face, the little gauntleted hand holding an inlaid whip, making a *tout ensemble* that was as lovely as a picture; so the gentleman thought, for his exclamation, as she stood in the doorway, was a spontaneous tribute—

"A picture for remembrance!"

And years afterwards, in speaking of lovely women, he would bring up the apparition that enchanted him, as the most bewitching he had ever seen.

Later, as she stood in the same dress in the deep embrasure of the window, the light of the sinking sun playing about her, the animation the ride had given her, replaced by the finer fire of the brilliant conversation into which she at once entered with her vivacious visitor, "the picture for remembrance" was complete.

It is not wonderful that such attractions made her a greater favorite even than her reputation as one of the most promising young writers of the day; and, conscious of the pleasure she was giving, it was not possible for her to find less than the greatest enjoyment in society, especially when, as in that she entered in Charleston, the highest culture accompanied uncommon refinement. Familiar with corresponding circles in Philadelphia and New York, she unhesitatingly gave the preference to that of Charleston, a preference expressed again when, years afterwards, she was again a guest in the city.

No one who met her during the winter of '51, will forget "the fascinating Mrs. Neal," whose movements were paragraphed in the public prints, whose *bon mots* were repeated, who was always the centre of the most brilliant circle in the room, who seemed too bright and happy to know any thing of the serious and shady side of life.

She quite overturned the ideas commonly formed of literary women: so young, so bright, so girlish and *insouciante*, was this one of the editors of the "Saturday Gazette," one of its publishing partners! was this the stay, not simply of her venerable mother-in-law, but of others widowed and fatherless! was this the writer of wise letters to young aspirants for literary distinction! and, above all, was this the sad-hearted woman, already finding "the world recede," while she was fixing her gaze on the skies which alone were satisfying, unchanging, and eternal!

So society saw only one phase. Every week a long letter was read in the quiet parlor in Seventh street, telling "dear mamma" what the truant had done during the week since the previous epistle had been written. What visits and visitors, what rides and excursions, what gay gatherings in the evening, and what the result of her morning's occupation.

These mornings were spent in *work*, no matter how numerous and fatiguing the evening's engagements had been; and she not unfrequently went to two or three parties, or a social entertainment after a concert. Every morning she wrote, sitting as usual, portfolio in her lap, on a low footstool, in the sunshine of the south gallery; or, if too cool for that, by the crackling woodfire, which she considered one of the luxuries of this Southern winter, and an inspiration in itself, after having had all her life only the sedate Northern anthracite.

In these home letters there was an odd mixture of business and pleasure. In turn she would consider and provide for the wants of the family in Seventh street; and another, almost as much dependent on her care and exertion; and would give a faithful attention to the details of her business affairs. Her care, and forethought, and prudence, blended oddly with the graphic accounts of her gay life; her descriptions of society were like her talk, sparkling with brilliant *mots*, and attractive from deft and graceful phrase.

No bee ever made honey in the sunshine more industriously. She gathered material in her visits to the Orphan House for the most pathetic of her books, "Patient Waiting No Loss." She wrote descriptive letters for the "Philadelphia Bulletin;" she kept up her engagement with Mr. Godey; wrote constantly for her own paper; and, when this was done, gave morning after morning to fresh creations, as if she could not sufficiently fill up her time, and idleness or even rest were impossible to her.

Her little nephew, a child of three years, was her playfellow when work was over: she rhymed and sang for him, and every evening, no matter what its hours held for her of social excitement, the child went to sleep with her songs lulling him, or her stories following him into his dreams. Time spent by others at the toilette, was not needed by her in her simple adorning; and often the carriage at the door would find her still in the nursery with the boy. "Aunt Lallish" was sweeter to her than any greeting "Mrs. Neal" received.

Though she had not time, nor did she dare to use her eyes for fine needle-work, she had a dainty use of the needle. She one morning brought her sister a baby's robe, exquisitely made, which had occupied her during stolen hours.

"When *did* you find time for this, Alice?"

"Oh, I made time, as anybody does who particularly wants it. I find time for all I have to do, though I am not as swift as you are in my movements, and have a habit of taking my coffee when you are thinking of ringing for lunch. I must own to the complacency with which I regard this exploit; I am as much surprised and delighted with myself as I would be with you if you had written a book. Won't baby's dimpled shoulders and arms be lovely in this; I kept thinking of that all the time."

She had great pleasure in the fine chimes of St. Michael's and St. Philip's, which made the city atmosphere ripple with music on the Sunday afternoons. Nowhere were bells sweeter than in this river-environed city; and Alice's first realization of the capacity of chimes was here. Her sister finding her in the open gallery one afternoon, apparently lost in the delicious harmonies, said:

"Are you making a worship of your enjoyment, and not going to evening service?"

"Most certainly I am going to evening service. Music like this makes me devotional; but I need something more than this to go through the week with."

"What do you mean?"

"Oh, I need to be strengthened all the time. This only soothes, makes me grateful, perhaps; but my life is *such* a struggle, such a fight with temptations; and then I must be made contrite for wherein I come short of the requirement."

The disposition to indulge in rest in the afternoon of Sunday, was often alluded to with pain; and busy as was every week day, she never allowed herself the indulgence without putting it down as "a yielding to temptation." While she had strength for it, she was in the habit of attending every public service of the day, and through the week, during Lent; and at other times she was always glad when it was said to her, "*Let us go up to the House of God.*" Certainly her "delight was in its courts."

Her fondness for statistical information was manifested in Charleston. This was her first experience of Southern life, and she made no superficial observations, but examined for herself into details that few women consider. She filled many sheets with the result of her investigations. When asked if she expected to write a book on the South, she replied:

"Oh, no; but I had an opportunity to learn this now, and I may have use for it some time; I never like to trust too much to my memory, good as it is. I believe I never neglect such opportunities—I never dare to. I've grown religious about that."

She found time for this in the midst of occupations which would have made twenty-four hours of daylight desirable. The secret of it lay in the directness with which she applied herself to whatever work was before her. She wasted no time in idle reverie; she thought and worked to the purpose, utterly intent upon what she was doing, till it was accomplished. She made a plan in the morning for the day's work, and lost no time in "drifting." This was not only the secret of large accomplishment, but of her work being well done when it was done.

In February she returned to Philadelphia, visiting Washington *en route*. She writes to her sister:

"—— —— is here, 'lobbying' I suppose it would be called, if she were a man. She is using all her cleverness to secure an eligible post for her husband. I have great faith in *tact*, and great respect for it; but when an ambitious woman is using it to push herself into a worldly eminence, you may be sure I learn a lesson. It is only another form of unscrupulous selfishness. Do you think I am uncharitable?—possibly. But be assured it is not the result of envy, as for a moment I feared it might be when I first realized the hard judgment I was passing. I only know my impulse was disgust; and I appreciated Joseph's shrinking from an acceptance of the many offers made to him of political position, or of advantages which his political services made it proper for him to accept, when I come to see what company it brought a modest and worthy man into!

"You laugh at my interests in politics, forgetting that I had some training from one who could have been eminent as a politician; and you ask me to write to you 'whether Millard Filmore or Fillard Milmore is President, and by what means he happens to be in the chair of State.' I understand what your affectation of ignorance implies. Do not be afraid of my knowing too much even to please you, who have such a horror of women dabbling in politics. If I had the disposition, Washington would cure me; but *what a place to study human nature here, where the eagerness of pursuit unmasks it so continually.*

"—— ——, the Massachusetts idol, is a guest in the same family with myself. I find myself watching him all the time, to see whether he is sincere. A man taking so lofty and pharisaical a stand is bound to be unfettered by personal ambition, or any petty influence from within. It seems to me a terrible thing to stand up before the world at such an elevation, that only a demi-god could fully sustain himself. South Carolina resents no man's position as much as this man's.

"After my little flutter in Charleston, it has been grateful to find myself in the shadow of stronger wings. Too much sunshine would be ruinous to me. I never should be able to save myself from a butterfly's life, and —*a butterfly's fate.* The world grows more and more unsatisfactory. Certainly I was not made for what is called pleasure, which palls so readily, that I am lost in wonder at those who make it their life; who have passed double my years in pursuing it here, and who must find in it a satisfaction which eludes me even on the crest of the wave."

## CHAPTER XI.

*THE STRUGGLE ENDING.*

THE benefit she derived from her winter at the South is evident in the different tone of the entries made in her journal on her return:

"This has been a happy Lent, so far. I cannot but contrast the bright prospects of this spring with the dark clouds of last.

"All seems too fair, too calm. I am looking daily for something that shall mar. I only hope when the trial of my faith shall come, that I shall not '*charge God foolishly.*' At present it seems impossible that I should ever doubt His care and love. Then, too, I seem to have no immediate temptations: home is so fair and happy, my days are so industrious and cheerful, my sleep is so sweet and sound. May God keep me from presumptuous sins."

March 24th she makes a sweet record of what she calls "a Sabbath-day's journey."

Her feeling, in view of the return of Mr. Haven to this country, was very disturbing. Her winter of absence from Mrs. Neal had shown her that in her extraordinary self-poise, "mamma," as she always called her, was cheerful, and apparently content even without her; too reserved, and possibly too phlegmatic, to make it known even if she "wearied" for the sunshine she could not fail to miss.

Then, too, another experience, which was not confined to her winter in Charleston, though its lessons had new enforcement there, made her reconsider her present position toward Mr. H. She had admirers whose name was *legion*, some diffident and hopeless, as became those who admired "a far-off star;" others, presuming and bold in the earnestness with which they regarded a possible future conforming to their most ardent desires. Her engagement, well known as it was, had not prevented some aspirations which annoyed her, and some whose sincerity made her unhappy, as she saw the pain her discouragement caused.

She writes on May 6th:

"I have just finished reading the life of Mrs. Godolphin. I do not know when I have enjoyed a book so much. One rarely knows so beautiful a character. There is much in the book that comes home to me now; her doubts, to marry or not to marry, for instance. I have quoted part of this in a letter to S., as expressing what I feel; but the struggle is ended for the present. I seem to have given up all to the direction of our Father, who knows what is best, far better than we ourselves can. I shall wait for some plain token. My husband will have more confidence in me, when he sees that I cannot desert a duty for a selfish happiness. All things now, as heretofore, will, I am persuaded, work together for our good.

"Another reason for liking the book is, the example of strict watchfulness and constant devotion which it gives."

"*May 29th.*

"This week of temptation and ill-doing is better than a deceitful calm—both the temptations that I most dreaded and most guarded against.

"Monday my devotions were hurried, because of business. I was successful, fortunately, but I was too tired at night to pray even. Tuesday it was business, and illness again gave me no time. Wednesday vain glory and egotism, harshness and bitterness of spirit. So on Thursday; still no prayer, no regular reading. Friday trifling. Saturday, was led, or rather, led myself into some of my worst faults.

"*Thoughts* to be pondered:

"It must always be remembered that consistency is essential to a useful character. Without it, many may love, but none will respect you.

"True humility, like every other grace, begins like a gift, and increases like a habit."

"*July 17th.*

"Though written months ago, this will do for the motto for my yearly review, to remind me in time to come of the principal virtues which I need—meekness and patience.

"It is five years to-day since my best friend died! Five years! Mamma sat here that morning, and I put my arms about her neck for the first time in my life, and said:

"'Don't send me away from you, mamma.'

"'No, Alice; you must never go away from me,' she replied.

"And now the struggle is always going on! God direct me aright, is all I can pray.

"Every day I find out more and more how much I owe to Joseph, and the trials that came through that love. He said once, '*We* will show Neelie a woman at twenty-five;' and to mamma, 'What a woman Alice will make!' I wonder if I have half fulfilled his hopes. Oh, may God guide me as lovingly through all the trials that are to come, in whatever shape they may be.

"Mamma is scarcely changed since then. Who would

have believed it possible! She loves me as well, or better than then, I know.

"'Mamma,' I said, a few days ago, 'any one to see me wandering around would think me very idle.'

"'No indeed, Alice; they would wonder how such a little body could attend to so much.'

"Dear mamma! I put it on record, not for the praise, but to recall your kind tone and smile.

"My faults of character have deepened, I fear. In some cases it is my fate to see the best, yet the worst pursue. I do hope I am gaining some ground against my besetting sins; but others have developed themselves, which seem even harder to watch against. I am less indolent, and more irritable; less selfish in great things, and more so in my daily life. I dread life as much now for its temptations as for its trials."

"*Sunday, July 25th*, 1852.

"'One temptation goeth away and another cometh,' says my invaluable Thomas à Kempis. This morning I have found these sentences almost as helpful, in the ninth chapter of the second book:

"'Temptation going before is wont to be a sign of ensuing comfort.'

"'Some comfort is given that a man be stronger to bear adversity. Then followeth temptation, lest he should be proud thereof. The devil sleepeth not, neither is the flesh yet dead; therefore cease not to prepare thyself for the battle, for on thy right hand and on thy left are enemies that never rest.'

"During this last week I have been much worn with nervous impatience and irritation. If I, not yet twenty-five years old, with so much health and so many comforts, say, 'Oh, weary life,' what shall I be at fifty or seventy, or with poverty, or loneliness, or pain; or what is to keep me in the endeavor of the intervening years?

"All last night this was in my mind:

"'If thou hast run with the footmen and they have wearied thee, how canst thou contend with the horses? And if in the land of peace, wherein thou trustest, they have wearied thee, how wilt thou do in the swellings of Jordan?'"

In the autumn of 1852 Alice accompanied her sister, who was awaiting, at the North, the subsidence of the yellow fever in Charleston, to pay a visit to some young friends in Accomac County, on the eastern shore of Virginia.

Her acquaintance with these young people was not yet personal, and had arisen in this manner: The "Saturday Gazette" had found its way to this remote part of the country, and fallen into the hands of a group of children, who were its eager and emulous readers. All of them in the end became writers. The eldest of them sent her first contributions, with a humble little note, to Mrs. Neal, the editor of "The Bird's

Nest." The sweetness and uncommon finish of the sketch attracted the attention of the young editor, who praised it; and in time, as more sketches and verses came, letters passed, and a strong mutual interest grew up between the little "Marie E." and her friend "Cousin Alice."

By the advice of Alice, contributions were sent by "Marie E." and her younger sister, and even a brother still younger, to "The Schoolfellow," a juvenile magazine published in Charleston by Mr. Richards. He soon shared his sisters' interest in the young Virginians. Since Alice Neal had first written to them, they had been bereft by death of father and mother; but they were still living at "Margaret Hall," wards of their eldest brother. Mr. Richards had visited them in the spring of 1852; and it had been arranged that "Marie E." should spend the ensuing winter in Charleston with his family, Mrs. Richards coming to Accomac for her on her way South in the fall.

This she did, as we see, Alice bearing her company. The visit was one of rare interest to all. "Margaret Hall" was a very old mansion, which had survived the flood so memorable in that part of the Eastern Shore; and its thick walls, arched doorways, and iron-studded doors, seemed ready to resist another siege of the elements. In this home, remote from all literary association, except such as their own household afforded, these children had passed years of mingled study, play, and romance, till when the two sisters were now just entering their teens, mere children still, their father's instruction had made them fine Latin and Greek scholars; and their well-endowed minds, with the sparse culture of a few periodicals, and some choice literary works which their father's library held, or which they procured for themselves in the occasional opportunities they had to send to the cities, were already giving promise of ability and productiveness. The third of this trio, the brother, whose clever translations from the Greek, when he was only eleven, had been welcomed by the editor of "The Schoolfellow," was destined to a short life of wonderful brilliancy—dying before he attained manhood, though not before he had graduated with honor at college, and had been admitted to practice at the bar.

The correspondence with these interesting

young people was three or four years old when this visit was paid. During this time "Cousin Alice" had been friend, counsellor, and comforter, and now she found herself looked up to with an admiring deference, as touching as it was graceful.

Driving over this beautiful country, wandering through its superb forests, visiting amidst its hospitable people, and leading these fresh spirits into new fields of literary culture, an autumn month sped fast for Alice. Here at last was *peace* after all the turmoil of the struggle; the world shut out, her soul grew strong. It was while here that she wrote the book whose material she gathered in Charleston. The preface of "Patient Waiting No Loss" is dated at "Margaret Hall."

"Marie E." did not go to Charleston. Circumstances developed themselves during the autumn which decided Mr. Richards to make the North his home. Marie came to Philadelphia with Mrs. Richards a month after Alice's own return, and at New Year's went to New York for the winter. Before a twelvemonth was ended, she became the beloved sister of her visitors during that lovely autumn—marrying their only brother.

Little did Alice Neal think that she was training a dear sister and co-worker in her young protégée; one who was to be a sister in spirit as well as name, who should stand beside her henceforth in all her work and life, ministering to her in the close of both; wiping the death dews from her brow in the final agony, and humbly and prayerfully ending the work which death found unfinished in the hands of "Cousin Alice."

## PART II.

# HOME LIFE.

# PART II.

## *HOME LIFE.*

## CHAPTER I.

### *SECOND MARRIAGE.*

*Jan. 1st*, 1858.

"FIVE years from the date of our partial engagement, we were married after dinner, in St. Peter's Church, Philadelphia, Fan., sister, and brother Willie being present."

This is the simple record of this event in her life. Mr. Haven had returned from California about a month previously: the entanglement of circumstances was such, that it seemed impossible to decide what would be wisest. Before this date there is a record running from the time of their first acquaintance, of the struggle "to know and do the right;" this struggle was making her life yet more turbulent and wearisome. Mrs. Neal laid no obstacle in her path; if Alice felt that she must leave her, she would spend her few remaining days with a relative, where she would have care and comfort, the inconsidered needs of an existence prolonged beyond her hopes, and holding little that was attractive in it now.

Hopeless of disentanglement, the knot was cut by the sudden determination that this life, "so hard and lonely," as she pathetically calls it, so wearing with its perpetual struggle, so full of temptations and trials, must *end;* that she must have the arm to lean upon, the judgment to guide, the ever present sympathy and support of a husband's protecting love.

On their return from church, on this New Year's Day, Alice, with Mr. Haven, entered the parlor which was no longer to be her home. Mrs. Neal sat in her accustomed place by the window, her tea-tray beside her, as usual, at that hour. Alice went up to her—

"Mamma, I have decided; I am Mr. Haven's wife."

The old lady said, quietly, though a little tremulously:

"You have been a good daughter, Alice; you will be a good wife;" and so she blessed her with unspoken words, each heart full of that which could not be uttered, as they recalled the former bridal, which had brought Alice to the home she was now leaving forever.

Some time after we find in her journal:

"Saturday we came to our rooms at the St. Denis, in New York, to commence the world together.

"For many reasons, our marriage seemed hasty and unwise. In the tangle of circumstances which surrounded me, I do not see how it would have been better to wait. I certainly believe our Father overruled all."

The next entry is:

"*Jan. 12th.*

"'*Continue in the faith grounded and settled, and be not moved away from the hope of the Gospel which you have heard.*' Do not let me, Oh my Father, forget the trials and sorrows of the past in this prosperity. Do not let my heart be lifted up to forget that it is thy gift. Save me from worldliness and insincerity, from neglecting any talent, any spiritual for any worldly pleasure. Help me to pray constantly for my husband's best good, to look forward with cheerfulness and resignation to the events of the future. Make me more humble, patient, and peaceable; more like my Master."

"13*th.*

"'*Beware lest any man spoil you through philosophy and vain deceit, after the traditions of men, after the rudiments of the world, and not after Christ.*'

"Help me, Oh Father, to repeat the prayer; to follow not the example of the world, but Christ's, in doing whatsoever my hand finds to do with all my might; in *living* a good example to those who do not recognize Thee as Master and Pattern."

"14*th.*

"'*If, then, you be risen with Christ, seek those things which are above.*'

"'*He that followeth after me, walketh not in darkness, saith the Lord.*'

"These are the words of Christ, by which we are admonished that we ought to imitate His life and manners, if ever we would be truly enlightened, and delivered from all blindness of heart."—Thomas a Kempis.

"15*th.*

"'*Forbearing one another, and forgiving one another, even as Christ forgave you.*'"

"16*th.*

"'*And above all things, put on Charity, which is the bond of perfectness.*'

"We are all frail: but remember, none more frail

than thyself. If thou shouldst see another sin openly, yet oughtest thou not to esteem thyself better than he."

"17*th.*

"'*Continue in prayer, and watch in the same with thanksgiving.*'"

"18*th.*

"'*Ye turned to God from idols, to serve the living God.*' The dearest idol I have known."

This little insight into the inner life of Mrs. Haven needs but a word of explanation. Mr. Haven was completely a man of the world, with no sympathy in the religious life of his wife. That she began to see the new forms in which temptations were to come to her, these passages of Scripture, which were doubtless significant of each day's experience, plainly show. She was at once on her guard against the onsets which her faith was to receive, and determined, by God's help, to maintain her ground, "*putting on charity, which is the bond of perfectness.*"

When they had decided to live in New York, she became an attendant on Dr. Anthon's ministry, but she did not feel permanently enough established to enter into any intimate church relationship. Their home at the St. Denis was, of course, a temporary one. Mr. Haven made his arrangements to return to his former business in Wall street, where he was a member of the Board of Brokers, and he embarked in it the capital he had brought with him from California.

Mrs. Haven passed her time in accordance with tastes which were too firmly supported by principle to admit of change. She wrote as industriously as ever, each morning, keeping up the various interests of which she was the chief sustainer: the household in Seventh street, Philadelphia, went on as usual, till it was broken up in the spring by Mrs. Neal's removal to the house of her niece.

Alice made all arrangements in business affairs as independently as before. Her income from her books and periodical contributions, amounting to twelve hundred or fifteen hundred dollars *per annum*, remained in her own hands, subject to her own judgment. It was distributed as before, with the utmost judiciousness. Thus at ease, and independent in her charities and good works, she felt, with gratitude, the rebound from the depression of the past few years.

There was one thing which was peculiar in this new ordering of her life. The world had lost its charm entirely. There was no longer any attraction in its gaieties or its pleasures. She rarely went out in the evening, even to a concert. Her sister was now living in New York, and her husband also had relatives there. These, with the friends who came naturally into her circle, made up her social life. A few (as has already been said) from the old literary cliques, whose brilliancy had fascinated her years before, were worthy friends of the worthier woman. Her standard was raised above the merely intellectual aspirations of those who failed to sympathize with her in her new life, "*hid in Christ with God.*"

There was peace, content, and with all, a fear lest prosperity should spoil her. This made her watchful and prayerful. How her prayers were heard and answered, will be seen.

In the spring of this year, Mr. Haven met with one of the reverses so frequent in Wall street. Outwardly, with no expensive establishment to be affected, this could not make much difference to them. Her tastes were simple, her habits of self-denial and industry undisturbed by her short respite from care. It was only in losing this, and in seeing her husband distressed and perplexed, that she could be affected by a reverse of fortune. They were looking out for a country home, and decided to spend the summer months boarding at Hastings, on the Hudson. In a cottage built upon a cliff, fronting the upper termination of the magnificent palisades, they established themselves with a content, on her part, that plainly showed how slight a hold the pleasures of life had in her affections. There was an Arcadian simplicity in their home and their manner of life. Mr. Haven spent the day in the city, as do most of the residents of thesc suburban towns; and his wife was glad and peaceful in her unvarying routine, her mornings with her pen, her work alternating with rambles in the picturesque grounds. The afternoon brought her husband home to the nest which held his treasure.

We cannot refrain from copying here a rec ord so private, that nothing but its deep significance and heartfelt sincerity could admit of its being given even to the world of her friends Her journal abounds in written prayers, the deepest feelings of her nature taking spontaneously the form of communion with the "Heavenly Father." On June 6th she writes:

"It would seem, after all, that my heart and life were not to be tried with prosperity. I grew daily more self-indulgent, and more dissatisfied with myself. It is good for us that we have been troubled, even for our worldly happiness. We are yet more closely united in our misfortunes. We begin to have some definite aim in life, and here, in the midst of God's beautiful creations, we think more of Him. Our time with each other passes pleasantly in our new home; our temptations to waste time are less. We have learned particularly our dependence on God, who is teaching us faith, patience, and humility, as well as giving us repentance for wasted time and means in the past, and resolves for better disposition of both in the future.

"I thank Thee, my Heavenly Father, for so hearing and so answering my prayer recorded in these leaves, even though it was made with fear that Thou wouldst withdraw the ease and comfort then enjoyed. It has been for the best for us. I do heartily acknowledge, and I would sorrowfully confess, that I have been guilty of murmuring, of faithless doubts of Thy goodness and care for us, of which I do earnestly repent, seeing even now Thy loving kindness in all that has befallen us. Grant that I may never be guilty again, through all my life, of the same error, but trust Thee in the future in all changes and chances of this mortal life, by Thy word, and by the experiences of the past.

"Help me to grow daily in holiness, patience, purity of heart and life, gentleness, self-denial, industry, and in every grace of Thy Holy Spirit, which I pray Thee to give to me abundantly, that I may serve Thee faithfully, and make happy my dear husband and friends.

"Give a pure nature, as far as is possible, to the unborn child for which we have so often thanked Thee. Bless it, I pray Thee, with a sound, healthful, and perfect body, a loving, humble, and obedient disposition; with as much talent and beauty as may please Thee, and be best for it in this world and the next. May it always be a comfort and a blessing to us, and may we have wisdom and firmness to guide it aright.

"For my dear and only love, my husband 'asked of God,' I crave, above all other blessings, a knowledge and love of Thee. Show him, I beseech Thee, that there is more than he yet comprehends in the life of a true Christian; teach him the one essential truth of life through the death and redemption of our Saviour; and that after this faith, and in consequence of it, comes the following of His pure example, not for a vague wish to be good, or for admiration of the excellence displayed in it. Help him to seek first the kingdom of Heaven, and add to this knowledge as much worldly prosperity as is best for us. Relieve us from the pressing anxiety of the present as soon as is best for us, and till then give him a cheerful and courageous heart, for the sake of our Saviour, Christ. Amen."

## CHAPTER II.

*NEW EXPERIENCES.*

IN the September of this year Mrs. Haven went to Philadelphia, to spend the autumn with her husband's family.

"There I was welcomed and cared for as in my own father's house; and, here my little son was born, on the 14th of October, healthy and beautiful."

Renewing some of the old associations, though quite out of her old sphere, life wearing a very different aspect, and bringing new and contrasted duties, the time passed quickly and pleasantly in her new experiences. But she returned to health and strength slowly, and to a resumption of her old habits of writing, with a consciousness of "baby's protest," which for some time interfered with her success.

She writes:

"I find myself waiting on him with a pen in my mouth, and get confused about my own identity."

"I feel a little shy in my new relation in the presence of the family; but sometimes I lock the door, and kiss my boy to heart's content. I cannot give myself up to this emotion before others; it is too sacred and absorbing."

Some verses, which will appeal to all who have had a similar experience, express this feeling. They floated through her mind before she was able to hold her pen; and though she never considered them worth publishing, they have their merit as an expression of the first emotion of the mother:

"I am thankful they have left me to a hushed and quiet room;
Its stillness is all holiness, its darkness has no gloom;
For nestling in my bosom, our first-born infant lies,
The seal of peaceful slumber pressed on his drooping eyes.

'Two weeks ago, my little one, thy first low wailing cry
Broke in upon a midnight hour of fiercest agony.
Hot tears of joy and thankfulness fell on thy upturned face,
For prayers and sobs were mingled in thy father's close embrace.

"That wailing cry, that thankful prayer, are echoed round me now,
As lovingly I pass my hand across thy cheek and brow;
My heart is full of gratitude, my eyes are full of tears,
To think the dreaded hour is past, with all its hopes and fears.

"God bless thee precious little one, most tenderly I pray,
And guide thee with a father's hand along life's weary way.
Or if His wisdom should recall the life He thus has given,
We then shall know a darling child awaits us both in Heaven."

Mrs. Haven returned to New York about New Year's, bringing with her a very beautiful child, whom she might well regard with pride and delight. In January a little niece was born, her sister's child; and the family literature had a curious addition in a correspondence kept up by the two mothers in the names of little Sam and Edith. The former, aged three months, was supposed to write a very clever baby letter to the week old "Edith Newcome," which was soon responded to with so much zest, that the correspondence continued till the death of the little girl, when something more than a year old. This "baby correspondence" was published in "The Schoolfellow," a juvenile magazine which had been commenced by Mr. Richards in the South, and was now flourishing in New York.

Mrs. Haven frequently contributed to this little magazine, which had now been for several years a favorite in various households in both sections of the country. It took the place with Mrs. Haven of "The Bird's Nest," and conveyed to children the interest in their young lives and experiences which she always felt, and to which she gave such charming expression.

She believed in juvenile, even in baby literature, and the venerable Mother Goose was an oracle with her. It was not to her "the intolerable *trash*" which some very sensible people call it. She said she remembered vividly the pleasure new rhymes of this infantile sort gave to her own little childhood, and she often made jingling contributions to the baby lore of the day, with the relish said to be shared "by the wisest men." Several years after this, when going to pay her sister a visit, she wrote to her:

"I shall carry a copy of Mother Goose with me, to help me win a welcome from your children. They are not well treated by you in this matter, and do not get half as much wholesome nonsense as they need—certainly as they would relish. I don't think I shall ever forget my childish satisfaction in the merry jingle, or the impulse these old rhymes gave to my wandering wits and my wide-awake imagination—perhaps, too, to my rhyming propensities. I would as soon withhold a rattle from a baby."

She kept up nursery fictions with graceful deference, giving them due place, as she always recognized the value of mental recreation in later years. Santa Claus came duly, as he does to all good children in New York and elsewhere. A rhyming letter of remonstrance, written by "Marie E.," in the name of Santa Claus, to the destructive little nephew, who was "Aunt Lallish's" pet in Charleston, amused Mrs. Haven very much, and was often quoted by her to other young destructives of the benefactions of the Christmas Saint. Her own pen was quick and ready to minister to the wondering children, and she kept in memory untold amusement conceived by the wit of others.

But, as I have said, this lore was not intruded out of season or order. It was always subordinate to the serious instruction which she never failed to have fresh and stimulating for the receptive minds of the young. It was to this the background, as were her gleams of humor and flashes of wit in her conversation, and it served to outline more clearly often the earnest truths which it was her aim to make impressive and attractive.

Children were a study to her. This is evident in the individuality of her childish creations. She never gave toys even indiscriminately, or without considering their effect; and Mother Goose was administered with as much discretion as Maillard's *bon-bons*. She saw the danger of inducing mental dyspepsia, by weakening the tone of the mind in childhood, too plainly to admit of her being injudicious. She did not even commit the common mistake of judging the digestion of others by her own.

In the physical care of her children, she was on her guard against the errors of inexperience; and she made faithfulness no less a duty dictated by conscience, than a pleasure taught by her affection. To no one could the cares of infancy have come with a greater sense of *onerousness*. They broke into an established routine imposed by a consciousness of obligation; they disturbed the nights whose refreshing rest seemed so essential to her health of mind and body; they interfered with her mental habits, and became, through all this, disciplinary to her spiritual nature. But they were welcomed, and, bringing their own compensations, she felt their value. Life was totally changed since Alice Neal had become Mrs. Haven. Every day she was less and less "*of the world*" which still environed her.

The winter after the baby's birth they spent in New York; but in the spring they decided to go to housekeeping in some of its quiet suburban towns; and, with this purpose in view, they made inquiries in reply to the advertisements of "country homes." It was already spring time, when a notice of a cottage residence in Rye township, near the Mamaroneck station of the New Haven Railroad, arrested attention. Mr. Haven could not leave his business to accompany her, so his wife went out of town alone to see the house, riding the twenty-five miles in a stormy day. The house was newly built, and had not yet been occupied; it was pleasantly situated in a grove of locust trees, a pretty cottage ornèe, apparently just the home they were in search of, and the place was engaged. She went over to Philadelphia soon after, to spend a week or two, and on her return was met by Mr. Haven, and conducted to "Locust Cottage," which, to her most delighted surprise, she found all furnished and arranged for immediate occupancy by his thoughtful affection.

In this pretty home she made her birthday record, on the 13th of the next September:

"This first birthday passed in our new home, was bright at its beginnings, and happy in its close, but made miserable through the day by my own fretful impatience.

"How much more happily we are situated than we were last summer at this time. It was then the close of our stay at Hastings, and we were to be separated for the autumn, while before me was the great trial of becoming a mother. There was no prospect of a settled business or a home."

She then refers gratefully to her pleasant visit in Philadelphia, and says:

"The following winter was one of ill health, discouragement, and care. In March, after many plans for housekeeping, we gave all up, and thought we would return to Hastings for the summer. The morning this plan was found to be impossible was very hard. Weakened by ill health and anxiety, I did not see what was to become of us—forgetting that our Heavenly Father had more ways of providing for us than we could even think of. Late in April we saw this house advertised, and I came out alone to look at it. I found a new, pleasant, home-like cottage. If it had been built expressly for us, it could not have answered better. It was a *home* even before it was furnished.

"I prayed God as I came out to direct us in our choice, and He certainly directed us here. We have had health, pleasant neighbors, and many comforts which we could not otherwise have enjoyed. We have had our friends around us, and so far have always been provided for, though there have been some anxious days.

"I must not forget to mention my short visit to Philadelphia in the spring, and the care and thoughfulness of my husband, who took all the burden of the removal upon himself, and gave me the welcome surprise of a home waiting to receive us.

"Baby's illness has been the great anxiety of the summer; but this is over now, and he is a great comfort. He is called very beautiful, and his sweet, patient ways make him very loveable. I am writing on the 14th, having passed yesterday, my birthday, in town. The fault of the day was, perhaps, allowed to me, as a landmark against the particular temptation and fault of my present life. Worrying over ways and means, fretfulness and petulance, God help me to watch against this temptation, and make me cheerful, patient, and humble."

In every trial that came to her in these new

experiences of life, as wife, mother, and housekeeper, she saw always beyond the pain and suffering, if such they brought her, the lesson God was teaching her in sending them. If she was sometimes rebellious under the pain and disappointment, she was oftener examining herself to see what good end He had in view, who allows no faithful soul to be tempted beyond its strength to bear.

Much of this experience, woven together by a thread of story, is to be found in a series of chapters written for the Lady's Book, and afterwards published in book form by the Messrs. Appleton, and called "The Coopers."

This volume is full of unobtrusive wisdom, sometimes dearly purchased by its writer, and therefore the more valuable to all making the experiment which now occupied her. It is this which commends it, rather than any special interest which attaches to the story.

Many a young couple has learned, from the experiences of "The Coopers," to avoid quicksands, to "find the leak," and to sail safely into smooth water, where the voyage of life can be made pleasantly and profitably.

## CHAPTER III.

### *IDEAS OF LIFE WORK.*

THE books which she was now writing for the Appletons, bear proverbial titles, as we have seen, and each one of them indicates the phase of life through which she was passing. She had written "No such Word as Fail," when almost heart sick with disappointment and discouragement; "Contentment better than Wealth," after "lying awake at night, planning how to get money, which was wanted for so many uses;" "Patient Waiting no Loss," when hope deferred made her faint with weariness; "All is not Gold that Glitters," as the illusions of worldly prosperity faded before her; and she could offer thanks to God who had given, and who had withdrawn His gifts.

These stories, save the titles indicating their spirit, of course did not tell the inward struggle out of which they had their birth, but the wisdom she was learning in the depth of the struggle; and God has blest their teachings to more than the young readers to whom they were addressed.

"All is not Gold that Glitters" shows more power than some of them. It is said to be wonderfully graphic, and true to the California life it undertakes to portray; and New England is certainly as well represented. The book has more scope than some of the others, and was quite a favorite with its writer.

When, from time to time, those who knew how much knowledge of life she possessed, and into how large a mould she could cast her material, and the ideas which grew as she wrought with it, would remonstrate with her for confining herself to children's books, and urge higher flights and greater breadth, she would defend herself with arguments that it was hard to gainsay, since they sprang from that which was noblest in her nature.

"A strictly personal ambition often stirs within me, prompting me to do as you say. Yes, I used to believe in my power, and picture brilliant futures; but I have come to have more respect for my little audiences than you seem to have. I write for the five hundred when you write for five; and if there is a lesson to be learned, it is better for the five hundred to be reached; so I aim at being popular, attractive, and easily understood, instead of doing more artistic work, appealing only to the few, though I know I do nothing for my reputation by these little water-color pictures, which, certainly, every one overlooks in the presence of such fine oil paintings as your ambition aims at. I have had my temptation to do as you say, and I have only recently been offered a large price for satirical society pictures, thus overcoming one of my scruples, which is, that I must make all the money that I can use; but I cannot bring myself to the work now."

A friend wrote:

"You could write a very brilliant society novel—no one could equal you that I know of in this country; and you do nothing with the wit which you have so plentifully at command in conversation."

She replied in much the same strain as above, adding:

"When I have nothing else to do, I will do as you

say. To tell the truth, I have planned such a novel long ago. I have refrained from using some very rich material in my stories for the H—— s, because I am reserving it for the book which is to come in some idle time, when no one is tugging at my purse strings, and my conscience is not pricking a moral lesson into my brain."

Keeping house on a narrow income, as they were doing at Locust Cottage, maintaining, with the income from her pen, the dependencies which she considered sacred, and pondering sometimes how to prevent the lightening of her home purse, she wrote " Out of Debt, Out of Danger." She was very methodical in her business arrangements, and she reduced household expenditure to a regular system, carrying out the proverb just named. Her precision and conscientiousness in the appropriation of her money is worthy of remark.

She one day opened a small drawer in her escritoire, and showed her sister seven or eight little purses. They had been speaking of the advantage of system in every thing, and especially in the use of money, and she illustrated her practice in this way, remarking:

"These all belong to different objects. I

never borrow from one to use for another, for fear that I might sometimes be tempted to be unjust. When my money comes in, I apportion it according to its amount, and these various claims which may be more or less pressing. M—— always gets her check every month. I do not even see it. It is sent by Mr. G—— as it becomes due to her, so I have no trouble about that. If at any time I have any thing left over, I put it into what I call my poor purse. S—— gives me a regular sum every month for the household expenditure. Sometimes, when he has had 'a good day,' he gives me something for my 'poor purse.'

"Once when our fortunes were at their lowest ebb, we chanced to have only ten cents in the house purse. Of course I do not mean to say that there was not a great deal between us and real need; but you know S. was out of business then, and I tell you of it to show how hard it was to resist the temptation, for the moment, to borrow from the other purses. But I waited, with a sure expectancy that God would provide from Friday till Tuesday when S. received a most advantageous business proposition, with a good income made certain. My *trust*, when I feel that I really exercise *trust*, is always well repaid."

Years afterwards she wrote of this period:

"I looked after every quart of flour, pound of butter, and beef bone. I knew just when every thing came home, what it was, how long it lasted, whether it went further than the last, etc. I defy any one to keep a more economical table, or to burn more cinders than we did, and yet we always had enough and kept warm. There was nothing belittling in this close attention to such details, for I was serving a large object and carrying out a good principle. Then, you know, my beloved expense book: every sixpence was entered, and S. posted it for me every quarter.

"One thing in your letter would trouble me, if I did not know it was false to yourself. You write: 'And so night comes with the comfortable and sublime consciousness of having "muddled" through another day.' You know very well that when you have been a good wife to W., a good friend to C., patient with baby and with the thousand and one cares of your, to you, very trying life, checked quick words and undue aspirations, such as 'turning yourself into a money bag,' for instance, the day has had its work accomplished. *Why, this is the sum of one's mission, 'taking the little foxes, and not letting them spoil the grapes.'*

"Now, see how little we know: if I had married a rich man, as you said I ought to, where would I have been? Of what use to myself or any one else? I *dote* on necessity: she has been a better teacher of philosophy than Dr. Wayland himself. It was rather mortifying, when I was first married, that I was not loved for being pretty, or for writing stories or books—only for being good! It seemed altogether too much to ask of me, with so much else to balance the scale! But no. If I wanted respect and love, I had to keep down impatience, and to cultivate domestic virtues generally. I began with that for a motive; now I see the higher one to which that was the stepping stone. So all aspiration ends in doing *to-day's* duty, and then 'something higher' is put before us. As Dr. G—— said to me on Friday: 'There is no *perhaps* with God. He is *always* ready to advance the faithful doer.'"

When her oldest child was three years old, she had three living children. She says in reference to this:

"I used to think I wasted nothing; but I must have wasted time, and my three children have been sent so close together to force me to find it out. I know that well."

What an insight into an earnest, faithful, self-denying life we find here! What a lesson to the many who admire such a life of beneficence, and feebly wish that God had given to them means to do likewise. Here was means commanded, strength economized and garnered, time almost created, and opportunity sought for. Nothing was petty and unimportant, as she says, that led to the accomplishment of her large purposes. Nor did she say "My work is done," when any one of these seemed to be accomplished, and so seek to release herself from the pressure she had imposed. There was always some one in her mind or her heart, ready to fill up the gap made by a necessity for influence or care in any direction ceasing to exist. She wrote to her brother:

"I have been intending to write to you for a week or more about ———, especially since poor F——'s death has left our hearts and minds comparatively free to think of one who is quite as near us, and in as great need of help in some ways. I have felt as if I have neglected him—not being able to see him, he has passed out of my mind, and out of my prayers, in some measure. Seeing this, I have just written to him."

Again, when changing one duty fulfilled for another, she says:

"This is less pleasant. We encounter stubbornness for gentleness, indifference (outward, I mean) for the affectionate gratitude for every attention he gave us; but duty is not the less duty, because distasteful. We have seen the result in one case—the miracle of answered prayer, and absolute conversion; let us take heart for this harder task, helping —— through the darkness, and uncertainty, and peril that surround him.

" *You* have personal means of contact. You can seek opportunity. If he avoids you, never mind about 'his place,' and 'your rights,' or how little your efforts are appreciated. If we wait to look after 'our rights,' we shall never accomplish any thing for any one. I don't mind his misunderstanding me, or even should I get it, which I never shall—real unkindness and ingratitude. The Example set before us for our life-work, always received both. We have no right to ask other wages. He gives them sometimes. He has done so of late, but not as our reward, only as an encouragement to harder, more regular tasks, undertaken for His sake, not from mutual kind feeling and benevolence."

To the same:

"You have your hands full, without doing any thing for E—— this winter. Do not let it harass you. I will give $5 a month toward her rent. It will be a great comfort in the end to think you have been allowed to help her; it ought to be now to you. Still, I know it is almost impossible to count blessings when trouble is hard at hand, and you see no way of escape. I know how, with my own strong and tried faith, my heart sinks at such a time; how ungrateful I have been in distrusting God's power and ability to help me, when man's help seemed vain. But I so often have had reason to say to S., 'Man's extremity is God's opportunity.'"

To a remonstrance at the amount of time she gave to her housekeeping, with so many other cares on her mind, she replied:

"I have had every thing to learn, and you know how distasteful such affairs have always been to me, when I felt at liberty to consult my tastes, or rather allowed myself to do it. I am beginning to take a little pride in my housekeeping. Mrs. Haven, pickling and preserving, is very unlike, I grant, Mrs. Neal, with a pen or book forever in her hand. I do many things in the store room and dining room which you were never willing to do."

Such household duties, with a not very expert cook, and at first a most inefficient nurse, gave her much occupation. Her failures, through her inexperience, were very humiliating, and she speaks of coming to appreciate household virtues for which she did not formerly have a due respect:

"I suppose, because people who are famous housekeepers are so seldom any thing else, and you know we grew up with a feeling of deference for mental culture, and of comparative indifference to these same housekeeping virtues, measuring their value as we measured mental growth, against the mere physical comforts of life. Do not imagine I am going over to the other side now; but I believe in doing every thing well that is worth doing at all. Bodily comfort and intellectual attainment still hold their relative position in my respect."

She wrote this to her sister, who was regretting that she was entirely shut out of the literary world in her country home, and her changed associations; and she adds:

"I needed the enriching which I get in my present life. I should have run to weeds, I fear, if I had kept on in the old routine. You do not know how my best life was sapped by that continual drain, and how soon I might have become entirely unproductive. I need the quiet of the country, the rest of these evenings which would seem to you so dull, the call to minister where hitherto I have been ministered to. My faculty for adaptation has its legitimate uses now; and in return I get a thoughtfulness and care ever present and *so refreshing*, after taking care of myself so many years."

The mutual advantage of their union she

often remarked, magnifying the blessing to herself. With all humility and a never absent sense of her own weakness and need of help, she became a religious teacher to one to whom she looked up with a wife's deference and devotion. Her anxiety for his conversion is manifest everywhere; and the fear that her inconsistencies are his stumbling blocks, keeps her always "at the foot of the cross."

In her journal she writes:

"I am learning lessons of resistance to despondency, but principally that I should pray as earnestly for my husband's best good, as I do for his worldly success. Yesterday, when my soul cried out—

'*Oh Lord, how long!*'

the answer came—

"'*Your Heavenly Father knoweth that you have need of all these things.*'

"'*Seek first the kingdom of God and His righteousness, and all these things shall be added to you.*'

"I never so fully felt this. We can pray for God's blessing on our worldly affairs, *if* He pleases to give it—*if* it is best for us.

"But for the rest, we are told to '*crave*,' '*seek*,' '*knock*,' '*importune*,' '*thirst*,' and we *shall* have, if the Lord will—if it is best for us. He *does* will—it *is* best.

We *know* it. We do not need resignation, except to await His time."

She one day checked an exultant remark made by a friend, with whom she could take the liberty, by saying:

"You think, as I once did, so much more of the top of the ladder, than of the foot of the cross;" and this remark expressed the wide difference which existed between the ambition of her early and her later years. Then she said, "I am fitted for something higher." Now she prayed, "My Father, make me worthy to serve Thee, no matter how humbly, so Thou wilt accept the service." She saw herself formerly in the light of her gifts and endowments, and through the medium of the world's praises; now it was in the light of God's requirements, and through the medium of His Word. Her successes are often commented upon in her earlier journals; in the later are recorded her failures and her fresh resolves.

# CHAPTER IV.

*THE SPRING IN NASHVILLE.*

R. HAVEN'S business engagements took him to Nashville in the fall of 1855. There was before them the prospect of a separation for the winter, and Mrs. Haven suffered very much from depression in view of it. The day after he left, the Publishers' Festival at the Crystal Palace took place, and she attended, with her brother-in-law and her sister, her husband having persuaded her to promise to do so. She was trying to divert a melancholy which oppressed her in spite of her trust and confidence in God, to whom she turned so unfailingly when clouds lowered about her.

The gaiety of this brilliant evening, where

were assembled the largest number of authors and men of letters ever seen together in our country, probably; where the sparkling banquet was forgotten in "the feast of reason" which followed it; where personal animosities were put aside, and the sneer died on the lip of the cynic; where Irving, Bryant, and other patriarchs, gave cordial welcome to those who were to succeed them in the world of letters; and the young gazed reverentially and lingeringly on those whose careers they humbly emulated; where the female writers received their own share of courtesy, and gave tone and softness to the scene, some fifty of them mingling with their benevolent patrons and exemplars;—all this, unique and brilliant as it was, made but a feeble impression on one who was eminently fitted by nature to shine in such a gathering. She could not fail to sparkle for the moment; but her heart was heavy, and only that which appealed to it was remembered. The record made by her of the evening is simply—

"The scene was charmingly gay and bright, but my chief pleasure lay in meeting some good friends, and in the enjoyment of the two Marys, who would not have been there but for me."

The winter held for her the trial of lingering ill health. She complains of a cough, sore lungs, and nervous tremors. It was not her first warning: eight years before she had had an intimation of her fate, though she says of it, with the flippancy of the age in which she heard the prophecy:

"When the doctor told me that I was threatened with curvature of the spine, and that he feared the seeds of consumption were already implanted, I laughed at it almost scornfully."

The time was past when such a warning could be thus received: she was becoming sensible of her want of robustness, and remembered with dismay her impatience of the wisdom which so long ago had bidden her "beware of great fatigues." In no part of her journal does she speak so humbly of herself, or turn more confidingly to the promise of strength from above.

Now, too, as always when her time seemed short, the claims of others pressed heavily upon her. With a friend of like earnest piety she made agreement to set aside certain days for special prayer for some who were very dear to them both. This had been a custom with her before this, and she continued it as long as she ived, with great gain, as she believed, securing visibly often what she called "the miracle of answered prayer."

During the winter she had great enjoyment in having with her, at the Cottage, her brother and his wife, her beloved "Marie E." Mr. Haven came on to spend New Year's with her, and she was especially glad in the unexpected reunion.

A variance existing between some persons nearly related, and in whose happiness she felt great interest, she attempted a reconciliation, in vain, however, and thus she received another lesson to wait God's will. She says:

"In all things this seemed to meet me: '*In returning and rest shall ye be saved. In quietness and confidence shall be your strength. In patience possess ye your souls.*' This last I did not understand so well. I know now that, weak as I was in body, and surrounded as I was by difficulties, my strength was *to sit still.* But, after all, their was little need of *patience.* My whole visit to P.

was marked by instant and almost hourly strength and comfort from above; and incessant battling with almost visible hourly temptations proved this gain."

At last the fruits of her labor began to appear.

"All goes right for Alice," said F——; "she will begin to think she has what she prays for more than ever."

Her throat continuing to trouble her, and making no gain in strength, she decided that she had better go out to Mr. Haven, in Nashville.

"There is room for faith" (she writes) "in this winter's journey, in my present health, and in the uncertainty of the future. It is the second time that I have left a home, and remembered that '*the Lord said unto Abraham, "Get thee out of the country, and from thy father's house into a land that I will show thee.*"' I find an old letter in which I went over the same struggle for faith in giving up my home with mamma Neal: indeed that was a much greater struggle. But this cottage is so endeared to us—our first *home* together, the birth of our little daughter, the baptism of our children, all that S. has learned here, and the many lessons and blessings that I have had, will never be forgotten. How gently the blind were led by a way they knew not!

"One thing more. Here I have been made to define

to myself my attachment to the church, and my faith in its purity; to love and pray for its prosperity, to '*lift up mine eyes unto the hills, and know that the hour cometh speedily when all nations, and kindred, and people, and tongues*,' shall be blessed in our Saviour's long reign of peace.

"This leading came in the shape of one of the most subtle temptations I ever was suffered to fall into, which I brought upon myself through spiritual pride, growing out of things which I have put upon record. Like my other temptations, it has ended in a blessing of strengthened faith and confirmed hope. The lesson of the last six months has been humility, outward and inward.

"Some persons are preserved in great temptations, and often overcome in little daily trials, that they may be humbled, and learn never to trust themselves in great things, when they are so weakened by such small things. Thou knowest not what is before thee in the way, therefore walk humbly."

She decided to go to Nashville by the way of Savannah, and arranged to sail on the 27th of February.

"Looking into Bogatsky for a text for the day, I found '*Satan hath desired to have thee, that he may sift thee as wheat; but I have prayed for thee, that thy faith fail not. I will keep thee in the hour of temptation.*' And the commentary went on to say, that though we were often convinced that a course of action was right and best, both by outward appearances and seeming indications of Providence, and by inward faith; yet it might be only a delusion after all. Nevertheless, God would ultimately overrule all for the best.

"More than once I had the feeling that, in deciding to go to Nashville, I was acting merely on my own judgment and wishes, and not following God's direction."

She then draws pictures of what she fancied might be their life in her new home, in which may be detected a little weariness with the quiet and impatience of the seclusion of her life in M——. It was in such great contrast to all she had ever imagined in her younger days, to be alone worth living for; even her sphere of influence seemed narrowing. In another place she might find a fresh form of social life, where literary tastes were more exclusively cultivated, and the mind would receive a new impulse; not that she in the least undervalued the warm, true, and dearly-beloved friends, whose affection gave her so much satisfaction at M——; friends whose loving sympathy followed and surrounded her in every experience of her after life, and who wept tears of unfeigned sorrow at her grave; nothing she knew could compensate for the loss of such friends. But the rich, brilliant tone, the fine *esprit*, which was characteristic of the social life she had known in the cities, was necessarily wanting in a country home, and she felt the need of it, at least the craving for it, which those who are brought from high living to a plainer, though it may be a more wholesome diet, will sometimes feel for the indulgences of which they are deprived.

She did not excuse or spare herself as she came to see the pictures with which she was feeding the old lòve, and which were alluring her from a home whose blessedness she had proved. She recognizes the "vain glorying" with mortification and distress, and seeks again the true light she felt safe in following. She was going to her husband, and their new life promised so much time together, "time always for morning prayers," which the necessity of taking the early train to New York sometimes made impossible at M——; then her health certainly demanded an escape from the rigor of a northern spring; and with these and other sober reasonings, she shut out the vain desires whose very remembrance humiliated her.

But she was far from happy, or at ease in making the change. Speaking of her voyage, she says:

"The sickness of my servant, of the children, and of myself, the confusion and novelty about me, kept me from the great duties of my life, just as the hurry and worry of preparation had done."

Of Sunday in Savannah:

"The heavens are brass; it is scarcely possible to pray. An impression of some coming punishment, some fall to my pride, hangs over me. I pray for it, rather than to go on as I am."

A telegram from her brother reached her; there was no trouble at the North; he had concluded to keep Locust Cottage for them, which was a great comfort to her. Still the presentiment continued to deepen, the foreboding of evil grew stronger. The next day a telegram came from Mr. Haven, saying that he could not meet her in Savannah, as had been expected, and this was followed by a letter giving her explanations. Without warning or chance of redress, the charter of the bank in Nashville, with which her husband was connected, had been repealed on the 29th, the day before the legislature of Tennessee had adjourned for two years!

"In one hour our plans were all ended. I was glad this blow had come: that I knew the worst.

"We started for Nashville at five the next morning, under the care of my cousin Fred. At such a crisis it was impossible for my husband to leave; but what a dreary journey was before me!—one that I would scarcely have had the courage to undertake, had I realized it before I left home. I was barely able to sit up through the day at home, and now I asked God for courage to live through the night journey, with the care of the children coming upon me, for my servant was a very inefficient woman. At midnight, sick and faint, holding my boy on my arm, and striving to endure patiently, the cars stopped to allow the train from Chattanooga to pass. I had not a single thought of expectation, and I could not speak for joy and thankfulness, when, in the dim light of a crowded car, I saw my husband's face bend over me!"

This spring spent at Nashville was any thing but outwardly comfortable, their stay was to be so short, and Mr. Haven was occupied only in winding up the business for which he was agent for New York capitalists; but one hope *was* realized—their children throve, and her health improving some, "was passably good." At this time she wrote to a relative at the North who was in much trouble:

"We are so apt to forget that God has more ways and means of providing for us than we can possibly imagine, it is, therefore, folly to seek to confine Him to our methods. I am reading Madame Guyon over again, understanding it better than ever before. I want you to have it when I get home: there are so many things which correspond with your experience in the past year, and the 'whys' and 'wherefores' are made plain. I can understand your Easter experience so well. S. says he would like to begin life over again, with his new views and principles. I would not. I am so thankful that twenty-nine years are almost gone; not for their worldly cares, I don't think so much of these now-a-days; but that 'the outward fightings and the inward fears' are so far accomplished. Sarah and Fanny, the 'Faithfuls,' go upward from the midst of the pilgrimage. But they are the very ones who are content to live and bear. Even the self-will of wishing to go must be broken. Do you know, I think self-will suffers more than any other sin? The horse and mule must bear the bit and bridle, while others are guided by His eye. I think that is the reason of many troubles that would otherwise appear to be incomprehensible."

Here we find the unconscious expression of growing power in her soul. The strength of her will was great, but her reliance and confidence in the overruling of God gave her the extraordinary poise which especially marked the latter part of her life. *She* was already learning the "whys and wherefores," which are full of mystery to those who close their eyes to the source of those influences whose operations disturb the course of our lives. She taught herself to trace clearly the hand of her Heavenly Father, dealing with her in love, even though the dealing came as a chastisement. Disappointment ceased to distress her; and expectation, crowned with realization, only filled her heart with thankfulness to God.

## CHAPTER V.

### *RETURN TO THE NORTH.*

THEY left Nashville in April, intending to visit Niagara on their way home, instead of coming by the most direct route. Mrs. Haven had never visited the Falls, and she anticipated it with great pleasure. Her health was such, however, that she knew if she did not go to Philadelphia now, she would not be able to do so for some time to come, and she did not like the idea of not seeing "Mamma Neal" for so long a time. Mrs. Neal was very feeble, but not more so than she had been for years past; there seemed no special reason why she should not live years to come. Still, the idea that one or another might die before a possible visit, as sailed Mrs. Haven so persistently, that she persuaded Mr. H. to give up the contemplated visit to Niagara. They therefore returned by way of Philadelphia, and Alice paid the visit which it was so much in her heart to make. She found Mrs. Neal appearing quite as well as at any time during the past three or four years. It was a great satisfaction to one who regarded her with a daughter's affection, that the unexpected visit gave the old lady so much pleasure.

On reaching home Mrs. Haven wrote to her sister that they had changed their route, because her desire to see Mrs. Neal was so great that she felt that, this ungratified, she could not even have taken any delight in seeing Niagara.

"It was impressed upon my mind that I *must go to Philadelphia, to see mamma;* so I said, 'the Falls will keep, friends may die,' and S. kindly, though rather reluctantly, gave up the plan, and indulged me in my own way. I enjoyed my visit very much, and shall never regret having made it."

Mr. Haven brought the letter in which this paragraph occurs, into New York to post it; and when it reached its destination, on the outside was written in his hand writing:

"A telegram has just came from Philadelphia. Mrs. Neal has had a paralytic stroke, and is thought to be dying."

Here seemed to be the key to the presentiment whose expression was so remarkable in the letter.

Mrs. Haven hastened at once to Philadelphia, but too late. The visit so insisted upon by her was the last interview with her kind friend, her "dear mamma," who had so long been looked up to with filial reverence. It was a great shock, and to her, in her state of health, a fearful one; but in time she could speak of it calmly—and she always reverted to that last meeting as a special guiding of Providence.

She says of her return home that spring:

"I think I never was so thankful in my life as on the night of our arrival at Locust Cottage—our own dear home—still ours unchanged. We went from room to room saying, 'Oh, this is so nice;' and it was doubly so after our uncheerful home in Nashville, and the discomforts of travelling. We were amongst friends too! And I kept constantly saying to myself:

'Oh how can words, with equal warmth
My gratitude declare.'

On the Thursday after our return, S. had to go back

to Nashville for a time. I parted with him with the most miserable forebodings. At night my brother came out with a letter and telegram, 'Mamma was gone,' and I not there!"

The summer passed quietly, and but for another great shock in the news of a fatal accident on Lake George, which occasioned the death of Mr. Haven's two sisters, the peace and repose of their home life would have been very favorable to Mrs. Haven's health.

On the 13th of September she made the following record in her journal:

"A busy day of household care, of weariness, and petty disappointment. The 12th had my birthday brightness. There were no visitors for the first time in two months, and I went to my room 'to gather myself together' thankfully. The quiet morning was given to looking over my papers—burning some, and thinking of the many things in the past year that were reasons for thanksgiving.

"My birthday morning was bright and beautiful, but my nurse was in town, so my household affairs were delayed; and I was wearied with attending to these and with the care of the children. This will, perhaps, be the trouble of the year, though far greater ones may be in store. Now it seems more than probable that with three little children, the eldest but three years old, such days will be more and more frequent.

"My text for the day was '*In Thee, the fatherless findeth mercy.*' Truly it has been so since twenty-six years ago to-day my father died. Twenty-three years ago to-day since I left my own, for an adopted mother; ten since the great change in my life with which this volume of my journal began."

"*Sept. 14th.*

"Yesterday being such a day, I am writing on the Sunday following. The cottage never looked more beautiful; the sky, the foliage, the autumn flowers, the softly tempered sunshine falling on the lawn. I have said to S. so many times: It is a Heavenly day,

'So calm, so cool, so bright
The bridal of the earth and sky.'

We read the service at home, S. still declining to go to church unless I do. The children are very lovely, and outwardly there seems no wish ungratified. Even the dark day to which I look forward is brightened by unexpected blessings. There is no flaw in the happiness of this.

"I find the same striving against, and yielding to, Sabbath weariness, even with so much to make me thankfully obedient; this, and cold, formal wandering prayers, are my easily besetting sins.

"It is afternoon, my boy and his father are going out

to walk—from the porch I hear my little daughter's sweet baby voice, the most loving, the dearest of little ones, shouting, 'Papa, oh, papa!'"

A picture of peace and content which might well satisfy one whose heart was uppermost, and attuned to a recognition of the mercies that crowned her lot. There was a deep peace overflowing her life; its fruits were budding out during the summer, in a work of which we find the first mention in a large volume full of memorabilia, such as she was in the habit of garnering up to use as material. In much that was left in this way we see the inception of work afterwards accomplished; but much remains unused in the life that was only too short for the work her busy brain had planned.

In the manuscript volume referred to, is the following:

"In wishing to give a devotional book to the servants, I have often been at a loss in the selection; most of the subjects are too advanced in Christian experience, or of too high a range of topics for their use. It has occurred to me to select a text and write a commentary, or perhaps a prayer and hymn for every day in the month, morning and evening—short, because of the numerous calls upon a domestic's time, and as simple as may be in expression and illustration. This I propose to call 'Higher Wages,' and to go on with it at intervals, as the business of otherwise wasted Sunday afternoons, when I am detained from evening service. Whether this plan will ever be carried out, I cannot say. This, by God's help, is the beginning.

'LOCUST COTTAGE, *June 15th,* 1856."

Following this are instructions as to where papers in reference to this work will be found in case of her death. When she had the book planned in this way, and for the class of persons mentioned, with the title of "Higher Wages," she selected references for the title page.

"*Know ye not that to whom ye yield yourselves servants to obey, his servants ye are to whom ye obey; whether of sin unto death, or of obedience unto righteousness?*

"*For the wages of sin is death, but the gift of God is Eternal Life, through Christ Jesus.*"

ROMANS, vi. 16th and 23d.

The first two texts selected for comment were:

"*Choose ye this day whom ye will serve.*"

JOSH., xxiv. 15.

"*I will give thee thy wages.*"

EXODUS, xxi. 9th.

Thus began a work whose plan and scope

were very much changed as she proceeded, until a book, "The Good Report," the last her pen was ever employed upon, was the result. Instead of being suited only to the comprehension of the untrained and ignorant, it expanded into a summary of the Christian's pilgrimage. There are forty days representing the forty years' wandering in the wilderness; and for every text taken from the Old Testament referring to this, is a corresponding text from the New Testament, confirmatory, explanatory, and exhibiting the harmony between the two, which was always a favorite study with her.

This, in time, became her best beloved work, and it contains every thing which could make such a volume valuable, as the product of a life rich in meditation and spiritual apprehension. She wrote and re-wrote, and revised with the greatest care, submitting the results of such earnest labor, from time to time, to those in whose exegetical ability and spiritual insight she had reason to place great confidence.

It is worthy of remark, that this book, containing from two to eight illustrative texts to each page, was written without the aid of a Concordance, she so literally "*searched the Scriptures.*" She said the time this consumed was well spent, since she found in the search so many passages that were of use in other places. Her remarkable memory was of course of great assistance to her; and her long-continued habit of reading daily, and of comparing passages, had led to much patient research and great knowledge. Her use of biblical references is always beautifully apt, often giving the happiest illustrations of their meaning. She says of this:

"I do not think I was ever a student of any thing but the Bible. To that I have diligently brought what was best in my ability."

# CHAPTER VI.

### *INTRODUCTION TO HER LAST JOURNAL.*

IN the spring of 1857 she opened the large volume which was not quite completed when she died. The introduction was a brief history of the progress she had been making in her spiritual life, which every year became richer and deeper. On the first page she inscribes for a motto:

**"God's Providence is my Inheritance;"**

the motto of Robert Dutton, Mayor of Chester, England, who, in 1604, stayed in the city through the fearful plague, though all besides, whom the disease allowed to do so, deserted the town; by this devotion he lost children and servants. Below the motto is an extract from a poem by Raleigh:

"Give me my Scallop shell of quiet,
My staff of Faith to walk upon,
My script of joy, immortal diet,
My bottle of salvation;
My gown of glory, Hope's true gauge,
And thus I'll take my pilgrimage."

From Thomas à Kempis, the following:

"There is therefore no sanctity if Thou, oh Lord, withdraw Thy Hand.

"No wisdom availeth if Thou cease to guide.

"No courage helpeth if Thou leave off to defend.

"No chastity is secure if Thou dost not protect it.

"No custody of our own availeth if Thy sacred watchfulness be not present with us."

There are great numbers of short printed paragraphs on the leaves usually left blank, very characteristic selections, some marking particular trials or events of her life, or special needs of her nature. They are evidently the accretion of the years which follow. Many more of these selections are lying loose through the volume, with here and there a memorial flower. The paragraphs are almost entirely of a religious character, and evidently were preserved because they were considered "helpful." She never allowed any thing to escape which would serve herself or others. The letters to her friends frequently inclosed such extracts, with a short note or comment doubling the force of the comfort or lesson conveyed.

"Gathering up the fragments that nothing should be lost," was a source of riches to her all the time. The same carefulness which prevented waste in her household, and which made her hold every possession as one who must give account, was a graft of principle. Nature had not made a "Martha" of her; grace developed in her the rarest combination of the two sisters, the careful Martha and the devoted Mary, which the world has known.

Here is one of the extracts which her own character might have suggested to another:

> "Charity is a virtue of all times and all places. It is not so much an independent grace in itself, as an energy which gives a last and highest finish to every other, and resolves them into one common principle."

The sketch of her religious life may as well be copied entire:

"Locust Cottage, *April 5th*, 1857.

"It is eight years ago to-day, by the church calendar, since the day of my confirmation. That was Palm

Sunday, April 18th, 1849; and in wishing to get the exact date, I am reminded how useful my journal has been to me in many ways. I am glad the habit was fixed at school. The teachers made a rule that each of the scholars should keep a journal. My first was a very childish and trivial record, showing, however, my peculiar traits of character much more plainly than I thought then. The next volume, written with occasional intervals of neglect, at New Hampton, exhibits all these faults of character deepened and strengthened by time. It ends with my engagement to Mr. Neal.

"The third was commenced as a record of that, and of the wonderful future which was opening to me through it. There are but few entries before his death. After this, it had a higher object. It became a kind of confessional wherein I accused, and chiefly excused myself in the folly of these years. Its chief value is the clear record it is to me of the change in the character witnessed against me in the first volume, and confirmed in that which gives the history of my girlhood. It is a plan of the battle I have fought, and I can trace some of the victories gained. There was no plan then. I struggled on blindly, with inward and outward faults and adverse or fortunate circumstances.

"The stand-point of this new life is nowhere written. It was an afternoon's talk with a simple-hearted, uneducated man who was going out to China as a missionary, impelled by a strong desire to work there. I do not even remember his name. For some reason, which also I cannot recollect, he called on my mother, who was engaged and sent me to him. I think this was in July, 1846. I am certain of the year, for it was shortly after the death of my adopted sister Louisa, which had made me for the first time very much in earnest.

" 'It would seem as if you ought to go instead of me,' he said, talking of his mission; 'you have had every advantage of education and instruction; I have had none.'

"I remember meeting all his arguments with great flippancy.

" 'Oh show me what this faith *means*, and I will be as good a Christian as any of you,' I said.

"I do not remember what his reply was; but whether from that or a simple inward conviction, I instantly felt that '*Faith was not of ourselves but the gift of God*,' to be had only for the asking. I went into my room, locked the door, and prayed for a full five minutes that faith might be given to me. I thought I would begin to read the Bible again, asking God to help me understand it. This I did more or less regularly from that time.

"In December of the same year, I came to Philadelphia. Party, opera, theatre, and concert-going followed, until sickness and death came. The inward struggle went on with more or less directness.

"The rest is in the volume commenced ten years ago and just closed. It is true that I find the record of Palm Sunday, 1849, the day on which I openly devoted myself to a better life. What have I done in these eight years? What have I learned? How much have I advanced?

These are the questions for to-day. In answering these my journal is of the greatest assistance to me, for it is in some measure a daguerreotype of the day on which it was written. I see through all, how my prayers have been answered, often to the letter—prayers that I scarcely felt, only knew that I ought to feel at the time. How all worldly circumstances have proved for the best for me. How my besetting sins of vanity and self-indulgence have followed me—how they have been checked here and lopped off there—how they have sprung up again when least suspected—what gain I have made over them, and how they perpetually follow me as 'spiritual pride' and 'innocent ease.'

"I have been reminded that inconsistency is a special work of the Tempter, inasmuch as it not only destroys the good we have sought to do, but hinders us from doing more, or attempting it—that by this we fetter our own hands against attempting God's service.

"The chief end of man being to serve and glorify God, how are we to do so?

"'*Therein is my Father glorified that ye bear much fruit.*'

"'*Every branch that beareth fruit, he purgeth that it may bring forth more fruit.*'

"Yet I shrink still from the pruner's knife, and the finer's fire. I never pray 'Lord humble me' that I do not cower and tremble in fear of the stroke, for I know that He is a faithful hearer and answerer of prayer. The great wish of my heart now is that my husband may be with me in all this desire of service and of increase of knowledge. Eight years this has been my prayer, 'Teach him Thy way.'

"Last Easter Sunday I felt beaten back. Still I did not despair. Looking to-day over the past four years, I see how great a change is already wrought. It is the '*ear*,' but let me go on hoping and praying for '*the full corn in the ear.*' I have commenced a solemn Passion week, with this in view, and the good of many of our friends. That I may be watchful, and faithful to my vow, '*Lord help me. That which I see not, teach Thou me.*'"

What can be added to this simple story of the grace of God working in her soul? The implicit confidence that her prayers were never unheeded, has the child-like character which carries conviction of its source and inspiration. Her nature was not marked by singleness, nor her mind by credulity. On the contrary, when a girl she was noted for scheming and planning, and for carrying out her designs with an amount of tact which was so unusual that a lady, who was highly accomplished socially, said, after watching her with much interest:

"She has every quality which would command success in a Parisian *salon*. I never saw a woman born out of Paris, to such an inheritance of tact."

This trait, so commonly misused in society, because used to further selfish ends, became one of her most adroit weapons wherewith to serve others, and to promote every good end and aim. She consecrated this as religiously as every other gift to her Master, whom she lived to glorify.

That she was not credulous was shown in the rarity of the cases in which she was ever deceived. She grew every year more and more astute, as well as more charitable. Her insight was such that evil seemed unveiled in her presence. Her own soul undisguised, compelled, as well as invited, sincerity from those about her. She was so unflinching in self-investigation, she so reverenced *Truth* in its every manifestation, that she "trod down" the old self "with words of shaming," lifting her eyes humbly to the cross from which she always sought strength and guidance.

Her filial spirit was marked in the manner in which she received what she considered chastisements from the hand of a Father whose wisdom and whose love she never questioned. She continually confesses to the involuntary shrinking of the flesh, for her courage was not instinctive; but the struggle is soon ended, and the acknowledgment, "*He doeth all things well*," is heard from lips still white with the agony she had endured.

Her journal is so feeble a showing forth of the beneficent action of her life, that the temptation is great to withdraw the veil her delicacy always drew over all the circumstances which involved the feelings of others. Where was there trouble or sorrow that her presence, her voice, her purse, or her pen could give comfort, that they were not offered with a spontaneity that showed them to be the offering of a heart in full sympathy? And in all, was seen the wisdom she had learned at such a cost. Every event of her eventful life had educated her for her work. Nature and grace alike fitted her to counsel and advise, to comfort and sustain; and she who became in the midst of most pressing family cares and duties, and in her delicate health, and dearly-bought leisure, the rod and staff of many a strong, but despairing nature, steadying the burden herself till the shoulders could take it again, was every day growing more and more "*like a little child*."

In a letter to a near relation, where her tenderness and earnestness make her eloquent, she says of herself:

"I am harsh and arrogant, and dictatorial by nature. Perhaps *you* cannot understand what I struggle against at every step of my own religious enlightenment; how often I am betrayed into saying, '*Lord, what shall this man do?*' But, dear W., it is Peter's zeal at heart. I want N. to have the inexpressible relief, the abiding rest and confidence in every trial, whether it is of God's sending, or seems to be of man's working, that this reliance on the love, the tenderness, the infinite friendliness of Christ has brought to me. No one but my Heavenly Father can know how often, on my knees with prayers and tears, I have sought this rest, this stronghold for her, when she seemed to buffet back the ministries of His Providence, when every thing seemed to be against her. Not that I thrust myself in to assume the burden of her cares; it has only been when she has talked to me of them, laid them open as one may to the near and dear, that I have said, 'Oh that she could take all this to Him, who alone could bear it for her.'"

Herein was the secret of her strength, her power, to bear, to do. This was the fountain of the waters of Life, of might and healing, which she drank from continually; and continually the power of God was manifested in her.

## CHAPTER VII

*HER SABBATH.*

PERHAPS no person who has had a religious education was ever free from the fetters which such teaching sometimes imposes. Reference has been made to the church connection formed almost in her childhood; from this she emancipated herself when she found that what should be considered as a stay and guidance was only irksome restraint. Whether from this time, when in her childish way she first sought to fit herself for a membership with the Church of Christ, and then as life's allurements opened upon her felt her resolution die away in the heat of the sun of worldly pleasure—or whether she was self-deceived in the foundation of her feelings, she certainly does not in her private record of them go back to that period.

She takes her first intelligent and comprehending impression of her duty to God, as we see, from a chance conversation years after, and she goes to the Bible itself to be taught. There were points in the faith of her childhood which did not appeal to her when studying out this matter for herself. She gave her confidence to no one, but blindly struggled through the mists and clouds which necessarily settled over her path. As her own strength failed her, she learned that from God cometh our Salvation. When human wisdom availed not, she went to the source of all knowledge; and as she read, her heart burned within her, and she knew Christ as revealed in the Gospel, and followed Him in the way. One by one, she settled for herself questions of duty, and her life made it plain that she came daily into a clearer light and a plainer path.

As years went by, she recognized the meaning of the teachings which had made so feeble an impression on her early years, and felt their value. She had became a communicant of the Episcopal Church, and was always a faithful adherent to its tenets; but her "true religion and undefiled" could not long be trammelled by sectarian influences. When her principles predominated over the tastes which were so much better satisfied with the service of the Church of England, her catholicity increased constantly. She always felt that in the bosom of the church where she had found repose and shelter, there was that which no other form of Protestantism could give to her at least; but she questioned no one's conscience who differed from her. Wherever the followers of Christ met to pray, there she could pray; informed by His spirit, she recognized readily the same inspiration in others. Her love and reverence for her own church was never less than at first, but her sympathies grew broader as she came to lay less stress on externals, and to remember, in all her judgments, what His would be who looketh at the heart and judgeth of the intention, "*trying the reins.*"

She said once that it struck her curiously in her review of the faith in which she had been bred, that she had to *re*-learn so much that she had heedlessly forgotten, or wilfully unlearned.

"I find out more and more my indebtedness to my Christian training, to the influence of the sincere piety of the relations who directed my childish thoughts. I have had many a weary step in seeking the old path. I have great comfort in *my inheritance of faith.*"

There was no doctrine peculiar to what is called orthodoxy, of which she did not make a study. She would sometimes say, "I have not yet examined this point, and have no definite ideas, but I will take it up immediately;" and forthwith she would apply herself diligently to a renewed searching of the Scriptures, and there would be an accumulation of evidence in her mind as passage after passage was found and applied, and the question forever settled.

She read very few doctrinal books; after "The Pilgrim's Progress," which she always said was next to the Bible to her, her favorite volumes were devotional. Thomas à Kempis was a daily guide. Taylor's "Holy Living and Dying" was always near her. George Herbert and Keble were great sources of comfort, and many more, Bishop Wilson of the number, were constant companions. She had also a singular fondness for religious biography. At first her tastes led to a selection of those whose morbid tendencies were in accordance with her own; but this yielded, as her mind took a stronger tone, to the healthier influences of sound thinkers and active workers. She could not have much sympathy with the devotee whose piety revolved about self, who spent her time in morbid self-questioning, her zeal in prayers in her own behalf. She daily and hourly illustrated her faith by her works, making the tenor of her life the most impressive lesson she taught.

She was once asked, "How do you find time to pray for all the world? I find it takes all the time and energy I can secure to pray for myself."

"If you begin by praying for yourself, it is very likely you will find time for nothing else; but if you remember others before yourself, you will be sure to find the time for 'Lord help me,' and feel your need so keenly, that this short prayer will comprehend it all."

Her ideas of a proper observance of the Sabbath, were the result of a close investigation of the most profitable use to be made of the day.

She interpreted the commandments as she did every thing in the Old Testament, by a comparison with the teachings of Christ. To those whose observance was less religious than her own, she was accustomed to say:

"I cannot judge for you, but I know my own needs. I know that there are none too many hours in the day for the rest from worldly care, and for the devotional service for which it provides me time and opportunity. I cannot believe my need greater than that of others; but I may be mistaken, so I do not judge for any but myself. One thing I intend to spare no pains to accomplish; the day shall never be irksome to the children."

In her journal she says:

"*April 6th.*

"The storm is so violent that I do not think there can be service. It was a great comfort as I woke this morning to think there would be *church days* all the week, that I could carry yesterday with me through it all.

"When not more than seven or eight years old, I used to wake with such a feeling of relief when Sunday was over for a whole six days, and I thought Heaven must be a dreary place when the hymn said:

'Where congregations ne'er break up
And Sabbaths have no end.'

This is a different feeling entirely. I am beginning to understand the possibility of its being Heaven for that very reason. We try to make Sunday a happy day for the children, for the remembrance of our own weariness which lasted so many years."

And then follows a passage comparing the way the Sabbaths were now passed by her husband, and his satisfaction in them, with those he spent when she first knew him—

"When he did not come down stairs till ten o'clock in the morning, and drove out to High Bridge with a sleighing party in the afternoon. Not very hopeful! God certainly saved me in the rash leap my engagement was. I often wonder at it now. He led us to each other for our mutual help and comfort. The necessity of watching my own conduct and consistency, lest I should put stumbling blocks in his path, has been of the greatest service to me; and his firmness has had the best influence over my waywardness. Yesterday certainly differed very much from that first Sunday of our acquaintance!

"Certainly the Sabbath is 'a sign between God and man.' They who hallow the Sabbath *do* win the blessing in spiritual if not in worldly gain, as was the old promise to the Jews. Keeping the Sabbath properly was one of my first strivings and difficulties, and I began to teach Sunday School only to keep myself employed, and so to lessen temptation. That first year of our marriage, *his* ways were so different; the whole year I grieved over unhallowed Sabbaths. Then we made a rule not to talk of business on Sunday. 'Never mind,' I would say, 'we won't talk about that to-day.' How many blue hours it has turned aside!"

The Sabbath beneath her roof was a peculiarly sweet day. The family arrangements were made as far as possible with a view to the convenience of the servants as well as their own. Such claims were never overlooked, nor were those of the children, although this was Mr. Haven's only day at home, and his happiness came before all these considerations. With what sweet earnestness and tact did she exert herself that all should say, "*this* is the best day in the week to me."

As her children became old enough to attend she sent them to the Sabbath School, though she carefully attended to the preparation of their lessons. She taught them verses of hymns and passages of Scripture, explaining every thing to them in the simplest manner, and often illustrating with her peculiar aptness and force. In the evening often, as they grew older, she was accustomed to gather them about the piano, and teach them little songs, leading their voices by her own; and as the nurse came for them one by one to put them to bed, her "good night" kiss had a blessing in it that surely "brought angels down" in sleep.

*Then*, she could consult her own tastes, perhaps some sacred music, or a chapter or two from a wise book, some religious poetry, the Bible, and so ended a day hallowed, and profitable to body and soul. She one evening said to a guest, whose fine singing of sacred music was a very great pleasure to her, in his occasional visits, "Will you read me my favorite chapters in Hebrews. You know them. Your reading of the Bible is a great satisfaction to me. I enjoy it as much as your singing;" and shading her eyes with her hand she followed the reader almost breathlessly, her reverential spirit making its own vivid impression in the sympathy it awoke in all in the room. So she hallowed the Sabbath.

She believed in the ministry of fasting to some extent, and writing of it in her journal she says:

"I have devoted this week to ——, in special self-denial and prayer. Last night I came upon this help and encouragement, if I dare take it to myself: '*At the beginning of thy supplication the commandment came forth.*' This is a familiar Bogatsky text, and was in the morning lesson of yesterday. In looking for it to read it over I came to this. I have never had any faith in fasting save as an exercise of self-denial.

"'*In those days, I, Daniel, was mourning three full weeks.*'

"'*I ate no pleasant bread, neither came flesh nor wine into my mouth.*'

"'*Fear not, for from the first day that thou didst set thine heart to understand, and to chastise thyself, before thy God, thy words were heard.*'

"It certainly has been so, from the time that I began to desire earnestly Him I had followed so long in darkness, but who had, nevertheless, upheld and led me the while. Will it not be so now?"

And here we find a hymn written by her for Palm Sunday, breathing a spirit of devout thanksgiving and praise:

Saviour, Thou hast gently led me,
  And my heart would grateful be;
Once I heeded not thy guidance,
  Now I press more close to Thee!

Then I thought myself sufficient,
  Then I thought my wisdom wise,
Knowing not Thy strength upheld me,
  Nor the blindness of mine eyes!

Thanks for every hidden danger
  Warded off by watchful guide,
Thanks for every block of stumbling
  Which Thy hand hath put aside.

That mine eyes at length are open
  To my weakness, to Thine aid,
That I heard when night was darkest,
  "It is I, be not afraid."

Save me, Master, or I perish,
  Darkness, death, are still abroad,
Still uphold me, still direct me,
  Let me not forsake the Lord.

# CHAPTER VIII

## *CONFIRMED FAITH.*

"Easter Sunday, *April*, 1857.

"THIS is not what I have been looking forward to as Easter Sunday. My first sensations on awaking were physical pain and a sense of lingering suffering.

"A gray, lowering sky, and an impatient spirit. As I came to myself as it were, thankful hope, peace at least, and trust were above all other feelings. It is the anniversary of the denial I seemed to have last Easter, which has been present with me all day. *That* was the repulse; the silence I had had before. Still I was not left to doubt that the answer would come at last to all I had so long prayed for.

"Now it is raining heavily. The day, after all, suits me better than one of brightness. '*Christ has risen indeed.*' I am grateful. I desire to be thankful as I have never been before for His precious death and burial, and

His glorious resurrection and ascension. My heart is keeping the feast, even through my tears. *I know in whom I have believed. I know that my Redeemer liveth.* I desire to be thankful for all He has shown me of Himself and His kingdom, here and hereafter, during the last week especially. He has rewarded my unfaithful vigil. It was to be for others, but the prayer hath turned to my own bosom. '*All thy promises are faithfulness and truth.*' '*He that goeth forth weeping shall come again with joy.*' This softly dropping rain shall cause the green grass and the flowers to spring up when the sun follows it."

She then puts on record some of the suggestive thoughts of the week:

"Death, the last birth pang, and so to be borne with fortitude.

"Mothers know most of Christ's sufferings; the apprehension, '*how am I straightened till it be accomplished;*' the agony, the support in suffering.

"Women not only 'last at the cross, and first at the sepulchre,' but the especial messengers to call men to '*come and see where the Lord lay,*' when they are faithful wives and mothers.

"Zeal and Love set out together: Love outrunneth Zeal, yet apprehension, a part of love, makes it pause and hesitate. Zeal presseth forward and seeth the burial clothes first, but love first *believeth.*

"Zeal is appointed to strengthen the brethren under

worldly temptation and suffering. To love is given the highest revelation of the life to come, the end of prophecy.

"Flowers a type of the purity of Eden, a pledge of the beauty and perfection of the new Earth."

["He that desireth to keep the grace of God, let him be thankful for grace given, and be patient in the taking away thereof. Let him pray that it may return; let him be cautious and humble lest he lose it."—THOMAS À KEMPIS.]

"*April* 16*th.*

"I have several times thought of a group of sonnets, to be called 'The Cradle and the Cross.' This morning I said to baby, 'that grateful little smile!' S. said, 'that reminds me of the chickens in Pilgrim's Progress, how they look up as they drink.' I thought of this afterwards. The helpless little thing knows my voice, and whoever has her, or however she may be carried, turns her head and smiles when she hears it. 'My sheep know my voice.' Yesterday this occurred to me. I take away hurtful, though most attractive playthings, and substitute those less desirable but safe.

"This was a comfort in Keble this morning. I have been so heavy-hearted at times this week: last night S. said, 'It is my turn to be encouraging—*Set your affections on things above.* Isn't that what you tell me?'

"'Revive our dying fires to burn,
High as the anthems soar,
And of our scholars let us learn
Our own forgotten lore.'

"Then, too, on a sheet of printed matter, which I was consulting about some business affair, I found that hymn of Uhland's:

"'Friend, thou must trust in Him
Who trod before
The desolate paths of life.'

"If these things do me so much good, why may not my thoughts help some one else? It is because there are such floods of weak, tiresome verses, that I do not write more; so many self-deceiving, that I do not want to be one of them."

"*April* 19*th.*

"The only thought that I have for my book to-night is not clear. Yet something suggested by the subject of the week.

"'*And beginning at Moses and all the prophets, he expounded unto them in all the Scriptures the things concerning himself.*'

"The necessity of our acquaintance with the Old Testament, not only in the way of example and encouragement, but to be able to understand types and prophecies as regards our Saviour and His work of Redemption.

"Again, '*Their eyes were holden till the breaking of bread.*'

"Often those who have walked with Jesus and learned much from Him, do not realize His presence till the breaking of bread, especially the Sacrament."

These scattered thoughts, and hints for thought, reveal what was occupying her mind, giving it purpose, and leading, in the case of material gathered for her book, to accomplishment. The group of sonnets was never achieved, though in the manuscript volume before referred to, are many thoughts preserved with the design of working them up for the sonnets. She judged, as we all are apt to do, of the utility of these thoughts and suggestions, by the service they had done herself. That which brought her help or healing she knew could not fail to benefit another. A "Common Place Book" could be easily made of "helpful" passages of prose and poetry copied or referred to by her. From some she extracted their sweet wisdom, and nourished and strengthened those who turned to her to be fed. With all she enriched herself, and provided for the demands she constantly received, to which so very few in this world are at all capable of responding. "Served herself by every sense of service rendered," to *live* and *serve* were identical in her mind. She forgot the *endurance* which in pain and weakness she could not but experience. She trod beneath her feet the selfish pleasures which are the sole object in life of so many of her sex—of all persons, indeed, both men and women; for of the two, perhaps the scale would turn more readily in favor of the self-denial of women; and all this she seems to do with the singleness and unconsciousness which guarantee sincerity. She nowhere dwells upon it; she nowhere exacts it of herself as one who wrestles with self for the reward of virtue. It was the spontaneous offspring of the inner life; the natural growth of principles so deeply implanted, so thoroughly inwrought, that you saw them only in their fruits.

Her beloved book had gradually changed in character and now in name. She called it "The Good Report;" its motto was "*A Good Report through Faith.*" She does not often allude to it in her journal, never except in the vague manner seen in the quotations already made. But there is another volume which seemed to be the treasure house for the wisdom garnered for her book. "The Good Report" became a record of her inner life, of her hours of meditation, of the comfort and strength which she drew from the Scriptures, in which she found the witness she sought of her Redeemer, and the promise of Eternal Life.

For years one wish, one hope, was deepest in her heart, nearest to her lips in the hour of supplication, uppermost always in her thoughts—the conversion to the faith and practice which marked her life, of one most near and dear to her. Many pages record the struggle, as "hope deferred" made her faith sometimes waver; and then follow the assurances which she repeats to herself, and which nourish her conviction that "praying breath is never spent in vain." Others whom she loved, many for whom she saw her friends interested, and for whom she prayed, came from time to time "into the enclosure of the church," and still she endured the trial of her faith; her husband, and her beloved, only brother, had never knelt beside her to receive the symbolic bread and wine.

"Once," she says, "my hopes died out, and a great temptation to distrust, and despondency overwhelmed me. Indeed, after this I had many such temptations."

She writes:

"One Sunday, utterly discouraged by a dinner table talk, I rose and left the table; taking up my Bible, I remember I came upon the text:

"'*We have toiled all night and have taken nothing. Nevertheless at Thy word I will let down the net.*'

"I came up stairs and prayed for help to do my duty by myself at least, and then began to write a chapter of 'The Good Report.' As I finished S. came up stairs looking for me.

"'Why do you stay up here in the heat?'

"'To keep myself employed, and from breaking the Sabbath.'"

A conversation followed, which, she says, gave her great chĕer; and not long after this, comes a record of a Communion service, too tender and sacred to give to others' eyes than those to whom she had opened her anxious, loving heart.

There seemed really now to have come a turning point in many things which had occasioned her concern; and she prefaces an account of some circumstances which made their future prospects brighter, with these words:

"How often have I said to S. '*Seek first the Kingdom of Heaven, and all else shall be added.*'"

As another Easter approached, she writes:

"This is, in all probability, the date of brother's Confirmation, and my mother writes me that K. will probably be baptized on Easter Sunday. How thankful I am that I took courage to speak to her last summer, else she would have been gathered in without my having 'part or lot in the matter,' when she belongs to me so nearly too! In her letter to me she says, 'I had almost resolved to give up trying, when you spoke to me. I have since thought that was the word in season.' Yes, and I remember how I delayed 'the word in season' day after day, and went to her at last, with so little courage. I *will* have more faith in these impressions for particular people."

K. was her young half-sister, the only child living of her mother's second marriage. Mrs. Haven had been a particular favorite of her step-father's, and was at home during much of the little girlhood of this sister. After her step-father's death she had charged herself with the direction and expense of K.'s education, out of love for the child and grateful and affectionate remembrance for the father. She constantly speaks of her as "my sister and adopted child."

Replying to her mother's letter she says:

"I do not think there is the least reason for doubt or discouragement for her. The settled determination by

God's help is the thing, and we have no right to doubt that our sins are forgiven the moment we ask for it in God's appointed way. Our natures still remain the same, only the principle of action is changed, a desire to do right, and a dependence on God's help, taking the place of indifference and actual wrong doing. Sanctification is another matter, and people are so inclined to confound the two. If people who have been ten and twenty years trying to do right, give way to temper or any besetting sin, a person just commencing has no reason to be discouraged because overtaken in a fault. They are only to ask *instant* pardon, not to let it hang over them as a discouragement, and ask more grace of watchfulness for time to come. Praying and watching with all perseverance, and the study of the Bible to know what to do, and to avoid, are at every stage of life the special duties, and the warfare with *self*, 'the good fight of faith' goes on to the last. Literally a '*warfare*,' with daily battles, losses, or victories; but this is all meant for K. herself, and what I intended writing to her."

"With K.'s letter, came a most discouraging one from Mr. H. (This was an old gentleman for whom she had a tender and great respect, but whom she regarded as in a fatal religious error.) We have been writing on the subject of the authencity of the Bible, and the Divinity of Christ, during the whole winter. The correspondence grew out of this: After poor C.'s death last spring I wrote him a letter, and remembering my cowardice in acknowledging the great principle of our faith—Christ the only way of Life—I spoke of it indirectly, though clearly. He replied to me soon after, and taking note of what I had written, said he had had to unlearn many things taught him in his childhood, such as the existence of a state of future punishment, the general deluge, etc.; in short, defining his religious faith as a simple belief in the existence of an all-wise, all-powerful creator, the supreme Good or God, and that for the future every thing depended on our reverence for Him, and on our good conduct.

"This last letter, after I have exhausted every argument in my power, is very, very discouraging. Were it not that '*the things that are impossible with men, are possible with God*,' I should despair of any change; but I know that the Holy Spirit is all-powerful, and that prayer *will* be answered, therefore this fast I keep for him and especially for Mr. F——. I hope it is not wrong to pray as I do for so good a man. It seems the height of presumption and of arrogance for *me* to think *him* in the wrong; and yet he *is*, if '*all Scripture is given by inspiration of God*.' What else can the whole line of type and prophecy of a Saviour mean? How else can it be reasonably interpreted?

"Another evidence to me of his error, is the paralyzed condition of his church: no earnestness, no vitality, no anxiety for the general distribution of the Bible, no earnest prayer that all the ends of the earth may have the Gospel, as well as ourselves. *They cannot love Christ as we do.* He is to them but a teacher, a perfect and holy example; to us He is '*God manifest in the flesh*,' dying for us, bearing our sins, our sorrows not His own, our Saviour, our Redeemer the Way, the Truth, the Life, the new and living Way, the only access to God the Father, '*Who loved and gave Himself for us*.'

"'Love so amazing so divine
Demands my soul, my life, my all.'

"A teacher cannot inspire this, a simple witness of the truth, a martyr. They say 'Socrates died more calmly.' How can they thus deny their Lord!

"I pray for Mr. F——. Here again is an impossibility, but for the all-powerful voice that turned Saul's Jewish zeal into Paul's Christian earnestness. I pray for him, because he has such a weight of influence with his friends, in his church, in the community. Once fully aroused, like Paul, he would sway all hearts by his eloquence and weight of argument, by *testimony*. If I am wrong in this feeling may God forgive me. If my motives are unholy, purify them. Let me in all things desire only the glory of God. Let this be indeed my chief end and aim, out of a pure heart, fervently. Now if ever, in the midst of such a general advent call '*prepare ye the way of the Lord*,' such miracles as these I seek, may come to pass.

"I scarcely receive an ordinary letter in which conversions are not spoken of. Father B. may be right. I said to him: 'When do you think the good time of the thousand years will come, father?'

"'In October, 1857, before the Indian Conquest, or the general interest in Africa, through Dr. Livingstone, or yet the bombardment of Canton; before the panic had fairly unfolded, or Union prayer-meetings were thought of, I said: "In not far from sixteen years, those who are living will see its commencement. I am bound to believe in it by every rule for the interpretation of prophecy."'

"'And do you think it will be a visible reign of Christ?'

"'No! My idea is that it will be a general preponderance of Christian principle, and therefore of the best good of nations throughout the globe.'

"If '*the secret of the Lord is with them that fear Him*,' father must be trusted with knowledge beyond any one I know of.

"At all events this has given me great help and comfort this winter—*to look for His appearing. 'My soul will watch for Him more than they who watch for the morning.*'"

## CHAPTER IX.

*LEAVING LOCUST COTTAGE.*

LOCUST COTTAGE was only separated by a hedge and a low growth of ornamental shrubbery from the grounds of one of the oldest residences in the township of Rye. The house, which stood upon a knoll elevating it considerably above the cottage it overlooked through the trees, was very unpretentious, but the grounds were lovely and threaded by walks, every one of which would have pleased the eye of the critic whose "line of grace and beauty" is so famous. When J. Fennimore Cooper began his career as a writer, "Closet Hall," as the place was then called, was his residence, and his first novel, "Precaution," bears that date. Closet Hall is still its name amongst some of the old county families.

This pretty place, whose late owners and occupants had become intimate friends of Mr. and Mrs. Haven, was very much admired by them. It was unoccupied now, and Mrs. Haven often wished they were able to remove to it. The feeling was appreciated and shared by her husband, who without her knowledge began negotiations for its purchase. She says:

"On New Year's day, 1858, we walked about the grounds, and S. told me for the first time of his losses during the fall (alluding to the disastrous "panic" of 1857), and said that the money he lost then would have purchased this place. For awhile 'we played at owning it,' and amused ourselves with planning alterations. But by and by we came down from the clouds, and home again."

This was written in utter unconsciousness of her husband's intentions.

Before spring, however, the secret came to light, and she was delighted with the prospect of so pleasant a home of "their very own." She wrote to her sister:

"In the winter it will be sunny and cosy; in the

summer with its trees, and its deep verandas, we can live out of doors in the shade. The low French windows in front open on a deep piazza, which is overgrown with roses. This was one of the improvements made by Mr. S., whose taste has done so much for the grounds, and whose ownership has very much improved the place, I am told. Apart from the satisfaction of having a home of our own—associations go a great ways with me, you know. Do you remember one moonlight walk through the grounds in the summer evening when the air was heavy with the perfume of the flowers, especially the tube roses, with which we came home laden? A few such remembrances will cure me of the spell the moonlight has held over me ever since those nights of agony during that first dreadful spring in Seventh street. I shall take nature back to my heart in our new home, and open to her every influence."

On the lawn each side of the house were clumps of fine old Willows. These now give name to the place; and after this spring we find her dating from "The Willows." There are few records in her journal which refer to the change. In her little business diary, a small book kept with more regularity than the journal, she writes:

"*Feb. 6th.*

"I gathered up the loose ends of business, and quieted my mind for Sunday."

"7th.

"Found it hard to keep from talking and thinking of the new home, but tried not to."

"8th.

"Concluded to take it, but I find it will be difficult to give up the Cottage."

In her journal she writes:

"*April 3d*, EASTER EVE.

"I am sitting by the open window in the delicious hush of a balmy atmosphere. A true Easter Even, hushed, watchful, but not sad.

"I have enjoyed my practice hour very much, and I begin to feel that I have more control of the instrument again. It is a great and fresh pleasure, and grew out of my determination to give half an hour at least of every day through Lent, to the practice of church music on the piano. I think so much of my improvement because of our Sunday evenings at home, and the more as the children grow older."

"*April 4th*, EASTER SUNDAY.

"To show how thankless our hearts are, I have absolutely to drive myself to make a record of the anniversary when my faith was so sorely tried, and which also saw it most abundantly confirmed. I looked forward to it only to find the morning distracted, first by a self-discussion about wearing a new bonnet, and when in church by the singing of the amateur choir, after all our week of practice. I record the evil as I would the good, nor is it a new thing to say how strange that the mind should be so distracted by trifles after the most earnest thoughts. These frivolous thoughts died away at last, and I prayed at least to be grateful for my husband's presence beside me. For K. and T., the first communion of each. '*Surely my cup runneth over.*' I had no time to write that day, and this seems so cold a record, so unthankful; my desires so much less earnest, my life so selfish, my aims so wandering!

"This may be the last entry I shall make in Locust Cottage. Four years ago I came out here looking for a home. What a home it has been, my journal bears record. Then we had one child, no settled prospects. Here we have gone through manifold chastenings and corrections, but all in love. Every day's journey in the wilderness has had its pillar of guidance, and its food from Heaven.

"In my reading during the whole week before S. was reëlected to the Board, I came upon many promises that the Israelites should enjoy abundance and plenty in the good land they had gained. Sometimes it crossed my mind that God was going to give us a worldly prosperity as well as spiritual gain; but I did not dwell upon it at all, though I remember especially noticing the cessation of manna, '*and on that day they did eat of the corn of the land.*' So it has been with us, since we have eaten of the corn, God's gift, as well as the manna.

"So far we have been fully justified in our decision in regard to our change of homes. 'The Willows' has been thoroughly repaired, and put in the nicest order, and is now nearly ready for us. Next Sunday will probably be our last here. '*If Thy presence go not with us, carry us not up hence*,' we have prayed from the first."

"*25th.*

"The last Sunday in Locust Cottage, where we have been so happy, and blessed so far beyond our expectations. I have seldom prayed for worldly prosperity, only for freedom from actual pressing care, never for a place of our own.

"Here I have learned most of what I know of God's goodness and love to us, *all of Christ* that I now comprehend. Here prejudice and indifference has been overcome in S., and we have commenced family prayers and dedicated all our children to God's service. Two of them were born here; all are in health; truly for ourselves we seem to have nothing to ask!

"Four years ago this month since I came out here, looking for a little sheltering home; how blessed it has been! I remember praying in the cars that God would direct my choice. I do not doubt that the prayer was answered. I knew nothing of the *way*, of *first* causes, or *second* causes, or the 'suspension of natural laws' of which people argue. I have no other argument than that of the blind man in the Gospel, '*This one thing I know, that whereas I was blind, now I see*,'' and that I did trust with implicit faith in God's guiding Providence, and every event of our lives proves that we have been led in precisely the way that was best for us.

"It seems scarcely possible that I am to pass through such heavy trials again in the future; these past few months have been such '*a rest round about from our enemies, outwardly in the body, and inwardly in the soul*,' that I shrink from the necessity of preparing for further conflicts. Yet I know such must be before me.

"I think sometimes that God has given us this new home as a trial of our submission to His will, when He sees fit to take it away again; or perhaps I may lose my husband, or——. But I thank God that it is all in His hands; 'I desire to be content to do Thy will, oh God.' I *rest* in the knowledge that '*with Him there is no variableness, neither shadow of turning;*' that He has said, *I will not leave thee nor forsake thee;*' that there is *no loss in Him.* The actual truth of God's watch care, and Christ's faithfulness, is like '*the shadow of a great rock in a weary land*.'

"Not that I should be sure of being so submissive and patient if the trial come. I know from my last week's experience that I am only good when guarded from temptation, cheerful because of prosperity, amiable when I can control circumstances. I am glad of the lesson, and of this morning's lesson, that I must learn to be content, to be counted least, and even to have failed when I am really trying to do my best. I see my temptations to self-indulgence in habit, and in spiritual self-denial. I plan much, but trifles seem to come between me and the accomplishment. I am silent when I might make an opportunity to speak for the good of others, and break down by my careless example where I have been trying to build up. These are some of the things I see, yet I believe—

> "In doing is the knowledge won
> Of seeing what remains undone;
> Let this our pride repress,
> And give us grace, a growing store,
> That day by day we may do more
> And may esteem it less."

She speaks here of sometimes allowing opportunities to converse with others on their best interests to pass unimproved. This was certainly a self-condemnation, like many others which she makes, which only a very sensitive conscience could have suggested. She employed many ways of approaching those about her, and every thing became an occasion for a good word. If she was in town and had business at her publishers, their testimony is that she seldom went away without turning to account some chance to utter a word in season. "She seldom went away without my feeling that I was the gainer by her visit," said one; and another remarked: "When she closed the door the sun seemed to have gone under a cloud."

In her home, if a servant spoke impertinently, or gave way to ill-temper, she was accustomed to say:

"I cannot talk to you now, when you are angry; go and say your prayers and then we will talk this matter over."

And said one who bore this witness to the grace of her beloved mistress after many years of service:

"I used to be angry very often, ma'am, for I have a quick temper, but Mrs. Haven never lost her own temper; and I would come back so ashamed after saying my prayers, that she found me quite ready to listen to her, and it did seem she might be growing proud-like that I was getting humble at last, and more patient."

If no occasion should come for a serious word which it might be on her mind to say to a guest, during a visit, the visitor would find on departing a note slipped into the hand with the "good-bye" clasp, or the same would take place when exchanging greetings on leaving church, as is the habit with country families. These expressions were not the result of sudden impulses, but of earnest and prayerful interest, accumulating for days, and months even, during which her anxiety for her friend would sometimes keep her wakeful and prayerful during the night watches. She once wrote to a very intimate friend:

"I do not know how I should bear the almost painful interest which I feel in ——— if I could not carry the whole matter to God, and leave it with humble trust in His hands. It is such an inexpressible relief to feel, in my own helplessness, that there is One, who is all-powerful, and who has promised to hear and answer prayer. I think if I could not feel this with all the assurance which the promises bring me, I should sink under the solicitude I cannot put out of my mind. Now I can do a little in my small way, but I have such a confidence that God can do all else that is needed."

## PART III.

# READY FOR REST.

# PART III.

## *READY FOR REST.*

---

## CHAPTER I.

### *THE WILLOWS.*

THE beautiful spring-time found them in their new home, the last and most beloved home on earth of Alice Haven. The strong attachment which she always felt for the "sheltering roof," and the abode of peace and comfort, sprung up at once in "the heavenly place," as she sometimes called it, which was now their own. In thick shoes, and a broad garden hat, she spent as much time as she could command on the lawn, under the old trees, training the vines and trimming the shrubbery, or in the recess of the grove enclosed by the carriage drive. To watch the light figure flitting about, the bright eyes, and still blooming cheeks, eyes lustrous now with the happiness of her daily life; it was scarcely possible to anticipate the actual future. But to her eyes there was a cloud, not yet larger than a man's hand, in the distance. Her perfect happiness was too much without alloy to last in such a world as ours. On the Tuesday of Whitsun week she writes:

"We have been here just a month, and are now thoroughly established. Every thing is bright and beautiful around us; the house, the lawn, the garden, are all in perfect order. I had made up my mind to have no carriage yet, but that too has come; so every thing happens to me—just as soon as I am ready to do without it, it seems to be given me. I am afraid of all this. It does not seem right to have no trials. I dread a sudden thunder cloud in my serene sky. So many better people toil a lifetime for nothing, spending their days in trouble and difficulty. Still a trial of my faith. I only see it in that light. Whether our hearts will be lifted up to forget that God gave it to us, and to neglect the increase of service to others which He will require at our hands, or whether we should be content to part with it at His recall.

"'In all times of our prosperity
Good Lord deliver us.'

And the closing verse of my morning lesson comes to me with a special significance, '*Little children keep yourselves from idols.*'"

She then draws a contrast between her life and that of a much-tried friend who had been bereft, within a short period, of family, fortune, almost of a home, and asks why her lot was so much more blessed, and how she could best make "grateful attestation" for God's goodness. Of her friend she says:

"She has honored her Heavenly Father, and proved that He is faithful who promised, by glorifying God in the fires.

"I say to myself, shall these things come upon me? I often picture myself alone, struggling on with ill-health; and I have exhausted imagination in plans to rear the children, and to provide for them. But I have the same promises, the same assurances that she had, and her example to recall, together with my own mother's more cheerful trust, more active charities, and more undoubting faith.

"'No change of time shall ever shake
My firm dependence, Lord, on Thee.'

"It so often rises up in my mind, my Rock, my

Fortress, my Defence, my Stronghold, to which I continually have resort. I like all this so much.

"I have had some special hindrances since I came to this house, growing out of the disorderly condition of affairs, and the difficulty of making new arrangements about the distribution of work, etc. The children took heavy colds and were all sick together; my time has been crowded and broken in upon, my prayer time stolen away, but God has been very good to me, and I am not left to the long-continued spiritual depression which I so much dread since my Nashville experience, and which arises from just such temptations, ill health, and in the commencement, over-confidence in myself.

"All seems prosperous now. We have all that heart could desire. '*Confidence toward God*,' dependence on our Saviour. Very little do we *know* of either, but we desire to know more. My eyesight (she was fearing gradually losing her eyesight), and the constitutional tendency to consumption, which S. has, are the only shadows on our path. So David must have felt when he wrote, '*The Lord is my Shepherd*.' How beautiful, how very beautiful that is! It is the only language which will now express my thoughts.

"Yet our present position is only a moderate competency; and there are many who would smile if they could see what I have written, and seeing my daily life might wonder perhaps how I could be happy, situated just as I am. I try to remember this when I am inclined to pity people in very humble life. I know a new piece of furniture, or a coveted carpet makes them as happy as our new home does us; and 'a whole floor to themselves' is quite as much as our house to us, long desired, as little expected, and as greatly rejoiced in.

"I did not intend to spend my morning this way, but in arranging 'The Coopers' for publication. It is my week's work, and I have not touched it yet. I felt that I ought to make this record. I shall be glad one of these days to have it, I know.

"I am reading 'Cecil's Remains,' and am delighted with it. Two thoughts especially please me thus far: Duties are ours, events are God's.

"'*What I do thou knowest not now, but thou shalt know hereafter,*' is the universal language of God in His providence. He will have credit at every step. He will not assign reasons. He will exercise faith.

"And if this should be my closing 'credit' to my Heavenly Father, let it be that '*Goodness and mercy have followed me all the days of my life,*' especially in the losses and prosperity of my husband."

When we remember that Mrs. Haven was the mother of three children when the eldest was but three years old, that she was always constitutionally delicate to fragility, and when we consider the constant demand made upon her strength, we can realize in some measure the amount of principle and of determination which was needed to sustain her in a life onerous enough without any of the business engagements which she so faithfully fulfilled.

When she was married she had little knowledge, as she confesses, of housekeeping, carried on with that attention to details which an experienced housekeeper bestows involuntarily. There had never been an opportunity for her to acquire this experience, and the work had no special attraction for her. In her Philadelphia home, order, neatness, and regularity prevailed. Her own large sleeping-room, her study, and the drawing-room were all arranged with feminine taste, and the daintiness instinctive to ladyhood But housekeeping with very young children, and a limited number of servants, taught her that to secure that pretty ordering of her surroundings in which she delighted, she must give a personal attention to which she was unaccustomed, and for which it was not easy to find time.

Order and regularity in the kitchen and dining-room, and the economy at first desirable in itself and always in its results, which made part of her system, could only be made certain by the careful oversight of the mistress of the house. All that went to the perfecting of *home* in its best and broadest sense, became her ambition. Immediately after breakfast her own hands washed the china and silver, and arranged the china-closet and store-room. Then followed the ordering of dinner, and the arranging of work for the day; after which she gave some time to her children until the nurse was at liberty to attend to them.

And now came the hours devoted to what was exclusively her own work. She was accustomed to close the door of her room and spend a half hour in prayer and reading. She often said that she gained so much by this preparation that she *made time* by it. She says:

"If I have guests I excuse myself for the two or three or more hours necessary to do what belongs to the day, as imperatively as if I were teaching, and had pupils waiting for me. When I have guests whom it is desirable to treat with more formality, I try to arrange to have little or no writing to do during their brief stay; but generally my friends appreciate my engagements, and are good-natured enough to occupy themselves during the interval."

Her habit and position in writing have been

spoken of; but one more peculiarity may be noticed. Her inkstand stood upon a little tray, on a chair beside her, if she were seated as usual on a low seat; she every morning put a fresh pen of a particular make into the heavy gold handle, worn smooth with its years of service. Her broad mark and full flow of ink did not reveal the fact that she kept only ink enough to moisten the nib of the pen, thus making necessary constant journeys to the inkstand. She explained this by saying she did her thinking during the time spent in refilling her pen. "Then with my thought clothed in words, I have no time to lose; so you see the rapid, business like erasure I make with a single line of my pen, impatient of the ill-arranged thought or inapt phrase."

Her writing hours rarely ended without great weariness and exhaustion, an aching head, and cheeks flushed to purple. She would sometimes take rest before, but oftener after the nursery dinner, when she made her own lunch. In the afternoon she drove, paid visits, if well enough, or paid attention to the seamstress, for whom she often cut out work. If she took this time for lying down, it would frequently be with a book in one hand and her watch in the other, lest she should forget the time, and not be ready to receive Mr. H. on his return from the city. For this she always made a careful toilet, and then the children, fresh from theirs, were brought to kiss mamma, and to show her that they were dressed with the neatness which would please papa. In all the years spent in the country, she never failed, unless prevented by illness, in this loving preparation for her husband's return. If the weather was fine, she met him on the piazza, if not, in the hall, with an unclouded brow, and a cheerful, loving greeting.

It is so often made a reproach to literary women that their houses are ill ordered, their children neglected, and their husband's comfort unconsidered, that too much stress cannot be laid on this trait in Mrs. Haven's character. A lady well known in the world of letters, who had been her intimate friend in Philadelphia, and who visited her in her country home, wrote to her sister:

"Alice, as you well know, was a remarkable woman. I never knew any one with so much literary talent who was so methodical and practical as a business manager and as a housewife. She would have put to flight as a false notion, the stigma cast upon literary women, that they are all poor housekeepers, and not very exemplary wives and mothers: in all these relations she was a beautiful model."

Never was a mistress more truly the friend and counsellor of her servants, studying their welfare with unfailing interest, and considering their happiness as well. The cook who began with her in her first housekeeping experiment at the cottage, held the same office in the household as long as her beloved mistress lived. She required the servants whose duties brought them near her or the children, to be well dressed and perfectly neat, and gave them means and opportunity to be so. She took great satisfaction in the services of one who was above her station in breeding and in education, whose pretty ways and delicate appearance were always a pleasure to her.

The same seamstress worked in the family year after year. She was always paid from Mrs. Haven's own purse, with the feeling that the wife of a man not over rich should either do her own sewing or provide for its remuneration.

She had a very decided feeling about the division of labor in a family, having little sympathy with the mistress who takes upon herself unnecessarily, duties that another can discharge as well or better, that she may thereby *save money to be hoarded, or to be spent in the purchase of luxuries.* For this reason there was always, after they were able to command it, a liberal amount of service, of the best kind, in the family, and this was amply remunerated.

The parsimony which denies this in a household able to furnish it, made no part of the economy which was, as we have seen, a virtue of the first magnitude in the eyes of Mrs. Haven. Care in the minutest particular consistent always with her general breadth of interests, a personal supervision of the most faithful kind, but never interfering with the discharge of other duties yet more sacred, and the closest economy that would admit of the largest amount of happiness and comfort, entered into the perfect system of her home.

# CHAPTER II.

*JOURNAL AND LETTERS.*

"*June 1st*, 1858.

"'THOU *visitest him suddenly in the morning and provest him.*'

"In reading 'Cecil' shortly after I made my last entry, I came upon this:

"'The Christian prays for fuller manifestations of Christ's power and glory, and love to Him, but he is often not aware that this is in truth praying to be brought into the furnace.'

"I have frequently felt this when I pray to be humble. I dread the answer to the prayer! I have felt that it was not best that all should be prosperous, without a blemish on our earthly happiness; and I have prayed that we might not be left to grow worldly, unspiritual, absorbed in the business and the pleasures of life."

Her health was again more than ordinarily delicate, a time of trial, and always great suffering to her was in the future, and she records with much abasement of spirit, the depression, and sometimes impatience, with which it affects her. Against this she constantly struggles, and prays God to help her. She writes in her journal:

"I am especially ungrateful, because a year since I prayed that if it were God's will, I might have a year of health and leisure to work; '*just one year*' I asked, and now because it has been granted me, I presume on more! This, then, is the cloud, the chastening I dreaded and yet asked for, and it is sent in the most gentle and loving way, so full of compassion as almost to take away the trial. As to the responsibility and uncertainty of the future, 'duties are ours, events are God's' let me remind myself. I have the same trust and promise for four that I have for three children.

"I know I always learn more in the seclusion I can now command, and I ask for knowledge daily. I have dreaded in my new home the threatened loss of the retirement I covet and enjoy; here it is, all arranged for me; my lessons are to go on, my time is provided, yet I hold back. Yesterday I was fretful and rebellious, to-day the sky is lightened, if not clear, and I write down this new lesson in self-knowledge, lest I should forget it and presume.

"I used to think I had real faith; I *have* thought I excelled in thankfulness!

"There is another thing: '*Little children keep yourselves from idols.*' My chief idol is bodily ease and comfort. Should I cry out because it is to be destroyed? I must learn to suffer and endure hardness; but I am so tired, I have had so many hard lessons! I am so tired of this perpetual struggle with fortune or with self. I dread lest the former should begin again, and for others. I am weary of striving toward well-doing; all that I have ever done seems so useless, and faulty, and worthless. I want to lay my head down upon a stone *anywhere*, and *rest* and *forget*, at least for a while.

"I deserve '*to be cast out again, stripped and beaten*,' and left to myself to take my own choice again, but I can only desire and pray, '*Cast me not away from Thy presence, and take not Thy Holy Spirit from me.*'"

Poor human heart! Poor, feeble, weary body! How pathetically the plaint is poured forth when the burden of life grew so heavy, and the hands so ever busy hung down, devoid of strength! The weariness which she had resisted so long, which *never* took the form of complaint to earthly friends, even when their tender sympathy might have drawn it forth, must find vent somewhere. Who that saw what she accomplished, and how apparently unfalteringly she walked along the roughest path, could know "what was resisted"? She sometimes says: "I have not much patience," or "I have little natural courage," but when in the life that was visible to others did either seem to fail her? To those who were anxious for her health under the pressure of such exacting duties and engagements, she would always write in the most cheerful manner, finding out every possible alleviation, and sometimes making the whole aspect of her life so bright and cheery, with such a golden glimpse down the vista of a possible future, pictured by her sweet hopefulness and trust, that fears for her would involuntarily subside, and the gloom that came with the vision of the feeble and worn worker in the vineyard, would be dispelled by the sunshine which was making ready the vintage.

Her power of consolation was very great, and it drew mourners to her as irresistibly as the fresh springs draw the thirsty. The consolations of Scripture promises were always ready; the possibilities which the merciful providences of God place in our lives were never wanting, or absent from her mind; and all that others had found helpful would come to her memory as she comforted and strengthened the mourning and the feeble.

To one dear friend she writes:

"I am sure from your letter that the worst of the conflict is over, and the hands of ministering angels are already bringing you 'the leaves of healing from the tree of life' for the deadly wounds you have received.

"Christian was faint and spent, you know, after that terrible fight; and where would be the victory without such battles? '*To him that overcometh*' the promise has been given; I often think of it of late, and of this—when I have passed through my hottest fights—'The nearer to heaven, the higher the mountains; *the deeper the vallies, the sharper the conflicts.*' I am sure it is and will be so. When we settle it with ourselves, and look for it, we are in a measure prepared for them."

And then follows a page of instruction and comfort from her beloved Bogatsky.

To another friend, whose long-continued illness had led to a peculiar and very distressing spiritual depression, she wrote:

"It seemed very hard to me that so faithful a soldier and servant of God should be left to feel, even for a time, forsaken of Him; but, dear C——, you can perhaps real ize more nearly than any of us the external agony of our Saviour's suffering when the light was hid from Him. If it is thought a privilege to know something of His lesser bodily pain, how much nearer *your* approach, and '*if we suffer, we shall also reign with Him.*' I am working away at a book of daily readings, called 'The Good Report,' its motto, 'A Good Report through Faith,' and the text for to-day, just written down, is, '*For He hath said, I will never leave thee nor forsake thee.*'

"I do pray, my dear friend, that you may be able '*above all to take the shield of faith, wherewith you shall be able to quench all the fiery darts of the wicked,*' for unbelieving thoughts are fiery darts indeed, and we know from whom they are sent. Do you remember Christian in the Valley, unable to distinguish his own thoughts from the wicked whispers of the Evil One, and so blaming himself bitterly for that sin of which he had not been guilty? I often think of it when the fiery darts are launched against me.

"When Christian had travelled in this disconsolate condition for some time, he thought he heard the voice of a man, as going before him saying, '*Though I walk through the Valley of the Shadow of Death, I will fear no evil, for Thou art with me.*'

"Then he was glad for these reasons: *First*, because he gathered from thence that some who feared God were in this valley as well as himself. *Secondly*, he perceived that God was with them, though in that dark and dismal state. And by and by, the day broke. Then said Christian, '*He hath turned the shadow of death into the morning.*'

"May this be your experience, my dear C. Surely

I, if any one, am bound to pray for it, when I owe to you the confirmation of my own faith, and the direction of my spiritual life; and I know that I am but one of many who owe their coming to the 'wicket gate' to you.

"I have read to-day, in an English paper, that Bunyan is really to have a monument, and in *England*, where he was a despised vagrant. I should like to give my mite towards it, for his book has been next to the Bible to me."

From her journal:

"Said S., as he gave me my month's allowance for the housekeeping expenses, 'Make good use of it. I have lost money to-day.'

"'I hope you will until you learn to thank God as the giver of every thing you have; to depend only on His blessing for success, and to give Him a part of His own again. He has given you a great deal this year. What have you given Him?'

"'Oh, no preaching! I don't care about hearing any thing more,' but very kindly, though I know he does not believe my doctrine. It is a great trouble to me that we cannot agree to lay aside a fixed part of our income '*as the Lord has prospered us*,' and yet I dare say and know that my greatest failures are not in almsgiving, but in gentleness, meekness, and charity; more than likely worse failings in His sight than the lack of some others in giving to the poor and ignorant."

"*Aug. 1st.*

"To-day has been brilliantly lovely; nothing wanting in sky or heart. It seemed like a birthday festival. When I knelt at the communion service, with S. one side and T. the other, I said, 'Here I am, and my sheaves with me.'

"When I asked myself, as I did continually through the morning, 'What is expected of me, for so much given?' it seemed to be, '*that ye bear much fruit*,' that I should strive to grow more Christ-like myself, and pray and work more steadily and abundantly for others whom I do not especially love, where the motive is more unselfish, 'to break a narrow will, and narrow prayers.' Lord, break them both, and give us all a new, deep, vigorous spiritual life.

"Yet the morning had its blemish in self-indulgence, in late rising and its consequences. The afternoon was marked by remissness in duty to the children, giving up teaching and instructing them because of their restlessness.

"Two lessons for remembrance.

"I am very thankful for the day, and for its happiness, '*a feast of good things*,' prepared and given to me without my planning or anticipation. This morning I could take to heart Jacob's prayer in my chapter for the day:

"'*I am not worthy of the least of all Thy mercies, and of all Thy truth which Thou hast shown unto Thy servant, for with my staff I passed over this Jordan, and now I am become two bands.*'

"I found myself saying a few nights since, 'Oh, I

read nothing now-a-days but books of devotion and a few novels!' I smiled, and so did S., at the connection; but it was true. When I read in my own room, I read to '*grow in grace and in the knowledge of our Lord.*' When I take up a book down stairs, it is for recreation. I have not had a thought of study or advancement for a long time, apart from my own pursuits. But I have asked myself, does not this demand of me other reading, am I not wasting a talent I should employ, and which I might fashion to the Master's service? Am I too old for study? I have never been a *student* in any thing but the Bible and its belongings; is it too late to begin now?"

Making reference to her social life in Philadelphia, her frivolity and gaiety, and her enjoyment in her successes, the remembrance of which frequently humiliated her, as it contrasted with the nobler aims and higher purposes of her present life, she says:

"I hope the fact that some know of it, here where, God helping me, I have taken such a different standpoint in conversation and action, will make me more humble and lowly before them. When I am tempted to think what advances I have made, may I never forget this!

"Last evening I began to read Bayne's 'Christian Life,' the introductory chapter, and then went on to his sketch of John Foster. This I noted as especially my own case: 'At intervals I feel devotion and benevolence, and a surprising ardor, but when these are turned towards substantial, laborious operations, they fly, and leave me spiritless amid the *iron* labor. Still I do confide in the efficacy of persistent prayer, and I do hope that the spirit of the Lord will yet come mightily upon me, and carry me through toils, and suffering, and death, to stand in Mount Zion amongst the followers of the Lamb.'

"And again his biographer says:

"'But he has made progress. A general belief in Christianity has become an earnest personal straining of the eye toward Jesús. Though all the earth fail him, and though his own heart harbors traitors, yet is there an ever-living Spirit of the Lord, and this can be reached by a mortal through persistent prayer.

"'*Not as though I had already attained, either were already perfect. I count not myself to have apprehended, but this one thing I do, forgetting those things which are behind and reaching forth unto those things which are before, I press towards the mark for the prize of the high calling of God in Christ Jesus.*'"

"*Sept. 13th.*

"In my reading and at prayers to-day I looked for a text for the year, for this is my birthday, and this seemed to be the answer:

"'*And He said unto me, My grace is sufficient for thee: for my strength is made perfect in weakness.*'

"It was not what I wanted to hear, for there is a foreshadowing of trial, and suffering, and endurance, rather than prosperity and joyfulness. Still I accept it. I believe in being directed to special helps in this way.

"Here is the text for the year: '*Be careful for nothing.*' If I had read Bogatsky this morning I should have stood by this, but I was hurried in the morning, and too weary at night. The next day I found what I had missed, this text, and what follows:

"'Always trusting that He will as certainly carry me through the difficulties to come, as He has done through the difficulties I have already met, so that I may even give Him thanks for it beforehand.'

"Many might think this a foolish superstition, but surely I may take the message thus doubly sent, and lay down all my care."

## CHAPTER III.

*RECORD OF* 1858 *AND* 1859.

REFERENCE has been made to a superior young person who was in service in Mrs. Haven's family. She was one of two sisters, both of whom had been educated in a *nunnery*, in Ireland. Unhappy circumstances in their home, occurring after they left school, determined them to come to this country and support themselves. After various vicissitudes, one found a home at "The Willows," till she was followed to this country by an old suitor, who persuaded her to become a mistress in a home of her own, which he provided for her in Virginia; the other, Delia, went into a large embroidery establishment in New York.

Having occasion, when going to the city one day, to take a message from her maid to her sister, Mrs. Haven was much shocked to find that a great change indicating failing health had taken place in poor Delia since she had seen her. This was in the summer of 1858.

Reared in comfort, well educated, daintily cared for as the girls had been, neither was fitted for hard service or close confinement. It was plain that consumption had marked Delia for a victim, and Mrs. Haven determined instantly that all that care and comfort could do should be at once given to the sufferer, with some hope of prolonging her life in a country home, and with the best medical advice; so she insisted on her coming at once to "The Willows," to pass the remainder of the summer with Annie. It was too late; the disease was firmly seated, and progressed rapidly toward a fatal termination.

The touching story of the sisters' devotion to each other, and of the closing hours of Delia's life, is told in the journal. For many weeks the two were together in this lovely home, where all ministered to the invalid; and both sisters, in their love, and their ignorance of the disease, were happy and hopeful. At last from Mrs. Haven's lips they learned the fatal truth, that hope must end, that death would soon terminate the sufferings they could not now remove, or even alleviate, and that only in God was there comfort to be found. To her, their best friend, it fell to comfort Annie in her great grief, while she pointed Delia to her Saviour. Both sisters clung to her as their only earthly friend.

"Delia, we will do all we can to relieve you; but, my poor girl, there is no help but in God. Try to think of your Saviour, ask Him for patience and strength; God will not let you suffer more than you can bear." And so the last hours passed away, and the death sentence took effect.

"*Sept. 29th.*

"This is a marked day with me. The shadow of death was prophetic. I have taken my first great lesson as to the absolute certainty of the sentence passed on all living, on my own unavoidable end."

Singularly prophetic indeed, was this entry!

On this day a letter came from a friend and relation, who had fixed on the next, the 30th, for a long-promised visit. Mrs. H. says:

"She was a person who would be particularly nervous, I thought, at the idea of death in the house. Yet it would be cruel to hurry the poor girls out of it. There was but one thing that I could do, and S. consented that I should go to town at half-past five in the morning, and make the necessary arrangements for them. It was gray daylight when I started, and scarcely more when I stood in the undertaker's shop surrounded by ghastly coffins, for any age and condition.

"The undertaker was very kind when I explained the case, and so was every one to whom I had occasion to go."

At ten in the forenoon she reached home, having travelled fifty miles, and spent two or three hours in the city occupied with arrangements for Delia's funeral, which took place at four o'clock in the afternoon, an hour before her friend was expected. The lady who was coming was one for whom Mrs. H. had a very great respect and affection; she was a perfect housekeeper, and this was her first visit to "The Willows." There could not but be a little feeling of pride, but there was far more regard to the proper respect due to her guest, and to her comfort, in the exertion made by the young mistress of "The Willows" during this hour for the reception of her friend, when, from the nature of the circumstances, the chief labor came upon her of arranging the house and restoring the habitual air of grace and comfort.

"At the end of the hour," she says, "I met the travellers on the piazza, with every thing outwardly quiet and calm; but what a day had this been since its early dawn!"

How illustrative is this incident of her active benevolence, her untiring energy and unfailing efficiency, and the regard paid to every virtue and grace which adorns life, by Mrs. Haven, a delicate, even feeble woman, whose life was already crowded with duties and cares. Prominence is given to this, one only of many stories of a similar import, because a curiously prophetic spirit, identifying the case with her own life unconsciously, made her keep, in this one instance, a full account in her journal of all the circumstances.

During the winter that followed her fourth child was born. Her health made it necessary that she should give up its immediate care, which was the source of great concern to her who placed so high an estimate on the privileges of maternity. Some interesting circumstances attended the christening of the child, to whom was given the name of one of her best and most faithful friends; but his infancy was marked by a much more than ordinary anxiety, as he had a singular tendency, shared partially by her oldest child, to hemorrhages—the slightest cut or rupture of the skin producing a fearful bleeding, which would last for days, and the child's life would seem to hang upon a thread. Mrs. Haven inherited from her father a nervous horror of the sight of blood. Yet it seemed to be peculiarly her lot to have to exert herself against this weakness, and "to charge her soul to hold her body strengthened" in circumstances when many women and even men with this tendency lose all control, and demand instead of paying service. No one not similarly affected could understand what she withstood in the case of this child, and in many more instances which were fated to increase in the latter part of her life. "Duty" seemed to give her iron nerves, and bridge over with these the "impossible" to others. No call of duty, not the faintest impression of it, was overlooked by her. Its shadowings were enough to arrest her attention and fix her purpose. And this was she who in her girlhood declared her revolt from the imperious rule of obligation! In her journal appears this entry, on April 8th, 1859:

"Sometimes the mind is impressed very strongly with a certain duty, as praying or working for the conversion of a person perhaps older, or in other respects wiser than ourselves, who has resisted years and opportunities heretofore.

"'Does God send *us?*' is the doubt thrown in as check. God is patient with the doubt, and brings before us such providential occasions or circumstances as ought to convince us that it is our work. In the first place we are to purify ourselves, and attack Baal boldly in his high places: we may ask others for help; as Gideon sent for the other tribes, so are we to seek the prayers and influences of those likely to be interested with the promise 'that where two or three are agreed as touching one thing,' to fortify other promises of success.

"Prayers are sometimes answered, and apparently denied because 'there are too many with us.' '*Lest Israel vaunt themselves against me, saying mine own hand hath saved me*,' and we are tried again and again, till our intention is purified, and all possibilities of self-conceit destroyed."

"*9th.*

"One of two things hinders our advance when we are

really in earnest and mean to give battle; a sense of our own inefficiency, resulting from real humility, or a discouragement thrown in by the enemy.

"God is patient with true humility: He encourages it. '*If thou fear to go down, though I have given them all into thy hands, if my word is not sufficient to give thee courage*,' we shall have even a new testimony, 'some news from the camp,' some occasion in conversation, or something that God makes use of to *prove* that *we* are indeed directed to work, and *shall* accomplish it. As to our insufficiency, see in Gideon's conquest, that He can make use of what He pleases, even the most trivial means apparently; 'the cake of bread overthrows the tent,' lamps and pitchers are swords and bows. It is *Himself* that does the work, puts confidence into the army, and we are to follow this up to victory. There are princes among the enemy. Oreb and Zeeb are taken from this humble beginning, or by this leader 'the least of his father's house.' It is not even strength, or skill, or courage that is to win, only deep convictions of duty, singleness of intention, and a simple trust in God's help."

Thus does she follow the leadings of duty, and fortify herself for her work.

In May, 1859, she had a visit from her uncle, Dr. Brown, whom she had called father since her adoption by him in her childhood. As she advanced in Christian life, a singular spiritual affinity and resemblance grew up between these two, each having such peculiarities of faith and practice, differing of course from differences of temperament and circumstance, as showed that their kinship was spiritual. A special sympathy and mutual appreciation had sprung up between them, as she came nearer him in religious growth; and his rare visits were times of extraordinary interest to her.

There is a record many pages long of their conversation on what is commonly called the second coming of Christ. How he interpreted the millenial period has already been mentioned, and how with her face turned toward this time of peace and joy for all the earth, and brightened by the radiance of the dawning she thought she discerned, she hoped and prayed for its speedy approach. She says:

"I am almost frightened when I notice how strong a hold this has taken in my mind. I seem to think of little else. I observe that as soon as I have read, thought, or watched much, these impressions of the nearness of the reign of Christ come. In the winter of 1856 this was especially so. But that was followed by such spiritual pride, and then such painful humiliation, that it makes me dread it now. And yet, as I have said before, '*The secret of the Lord is with them that fear Him,*' and who lives so near of all I know as father? There were Simeon and Anna who recognized his first advent at once while all the rest were looking for it in the future. He was thirty years *in the world* before His ministry was *felt.* I *must* believe that He is now at the threshold.

"And what good is this knowledge or this hope? It stimulates and cheers, *or ought to;* renews our energies more and more to gather *our* clusters of the grapes of the world's harvest, our 'sheaf of the wheat.' '*And when these things begin to come to pass, then look up and lift up your hands, for your redemption draweth near. Know ye that the Kingdom of God is at hand.*'"

In a memorandum of a letter to one of those persons with whom she was corresponding, on the reality of a work of grace in the heart, she makes her point, in its influence in the transformation of the individual character, and in our experience in the change in ourselves. She says:

"A simple faith is absolutely necessary, for Jesus has certainly said that unless we have the trust of a little child, who raises no cavils, and asks not 'why' or 'how,' but believes because his father spoke, we cannot enter into the Kingdom of Heaven. How can a child's feeble powers comprehend the motives of our restrictive government? Do we stop to explain to him? Can *our* limited intelligence fathom the Infinite wisdom? How are we to approach God? Only through obedience and belief. It is the work of Eternity to grow nearer to Him in apprehension."

In July of this year Mrs. Haven went up to Hudson to visit her own mother. While there she accompanied her mother to call on a very aged and infirm woman, a distant relative of her grandmother, who was now eighty-four years old. The visit made a striking impression upon Mrs. H. The old lady's life had been one of singular misfortune, toil, and isolation from her relatives; besides she had suffered for fifty years from a tumor on her arm.

"When she first came to our house, many years ago, I was almost a child. She was then a very old woman, wrinkled and feeble. My mother says she wanted to kiss me, and hesitated, fearing I would object; and then when I found it out I said, 'Why, kiss me, Auntie B.;' and that she had always loved me very much ever since that visit.

"I talked with her about her removal to 'The Old Ladies Home in Brooklyn,' as her home in Hudson was not a pleasant one. She told me the story of her long, hard life, of her trust in God, and her peace in that trust."

This long story was written out by Mrs.

Haven, and printed in a religious newspaper. The journal proceeds:

"After we were interrupted I went home with my heart full. I could hardly help crying in the street; but I had an engagement to meet K.'s music teacher, so I could not relieve my full heart even when I reached home. As I took my bonnet off I said to myself: 'Why have I youth, and health, and personal attractiveness and independence, when this good, humble, Christian woman, is so stripped and so desolate? Her little, loving child who seemed to sit beside her as she talked, and to look up into her face with wistful tenderness, even he was taken away from her; she does not know when, she has not heard from him for forty years, to know whether he is living or dead.' I felt choked with sobs during all the business conversation that followed.

"Once, a few days before I left home, when very weary and discouraged, I sat on the piazza, and leaned my head back in my chair. 'When I am dead,' I said to myself, 'I cannot suffer any more, either pain or care, and it is not worth while to live.'

"I did not say that I wished I was dead, but I thought death seemed very inviting.

"'There is one *sin* that God has mercifully kept me from,' said Aunt B. this morning, 'I have never been allowed to ask to die. I have always been willing to live if it was His will. I have never prayed to die, and I am thankful that I have been mercifully kept from it.'

"The self-reproachful remembrance of my thoughts that night, went through me like an arrow. I had a beautiful home, the kindest of husbands, loving little children and friends. She, worn out with years of labor and pain, with constant physical suffering, a burden to her nearest friends, and now to be sent away from them, to die amongst strangers; certain that death, when it *did* come, would be an entrance upon an affluence of life, and strength, and fulness of blessing, yet '*willing to wait.*' Oh, my God! what a reproach to my selfish, my ungrateful heart! What a lesson for the future!

"I prayed that I might never forget it. I prayed, standing up in my room, choking with those unshed tears, that God would so impress it upon my mind that I might never forget it, whatever I was called upon to pass through. I pray so now.

"'I remember,' said the old lady, 'once when your grandfather had been trying to reason with me, when I was in a great deal of trouble, how impossible it seemed to me to comprehend and to believe what he said. I suppose he went home and prayed for me afterwards, for that night I seemed to reach the light and Jesus, who had stood so far away from me with such thick darkness between us.'"

And now this fifty years afterwards this blessing is returned upon his children's children! Surely the generations of the righteous are blessed, and this blessing is a wonderful inheritance:

and how cheering to think that the efforts we make now for the comfort and conversion of others may come home to our own children yet unborn! So does every ripple of the pool of healing spread and spread until it dies upon the shore of Time.

## CHAPTER IV.

*WINTERS IN FLORIDA AND SANTA CRUZ.*

"*Oct. 7th*, 1859.

"IT is a bright, sunny, crisp October day, a cloudless sky, a low wind wandering through the still green foliage, soft shadows swaying over my window and on the green grass beneath. No frost yet, cool as the season has been, and geraniums, dahlias, and heliotropes are still flowering in the borders.

"A hard day for a death sentence. Yet death and loneliness hang over me. When I hear S——'s racking cough, shaking him from head to foot, a horrible dread comes over me, and my fears grow stronger and stronger."

The illness of Mr. Haven continued to increase till he was entirely prostrated by a severe hemorrhage, which made even his physicians give up hope of his recovery. A warm climate was advised, and they went first to Charleston, thence to Florida, where they remained till spring. The short record of this journey in her journal is made after her return. She says:

"I can hardly realize the deep waters of last mid-winter, the fiery trial we passed through together, the hardest of my life. Our only hope was a warm climate, and some of our friends tried to dissuade us from that. We gave up Santa Cruz because the yellow fever was there, and took the advice of Major Leslie, about Palatka, in Florida. On the 4th of February we left home in the steamer Columbia, for Charleston."

The separation from her little children, especially her baby, not quite a year old, was very trying; but they were left in careful hands, and with kind and faithful servants, she feeling it her duty to accompany her husband, whose life seemed almost to depend upon her faithful care. Her own health needed the change almost as much, but of this she did not seem conscious, though others saw it plainly enough. She says of their stay in Charleston:

"We had a delightful time, but my winter's work began to tell upon me. I took a heavy cold and began to cough, and was quite ill. I talked with poor Carrie C. about dying, little thinking that she was to go first."

They were obliged to decline many of the courtesies so abundantly and cordially extended to them by her old friends and admirers, who would gladly have made her visit a complete ovation, as indeed was the case in many places where they stopped, and met friends or presented letters. Everywhere her name as a writer, and her fame especially amongst children and young persons, had preceded her, and prepared a royal welcome for her. An extract from a letter. written to her mother from Florida, will give some idea of this. It is dated at ——:

"We brought letters to Mr. Fairbanks, the historian of Florida, a man of wealth and liberal views, and Mr. Miller, the rector of the church; but before they were delivered two beautiful baskets of flowers were sent to me with a card 'For Cousin Alice;' and when Mr. Fairbanks took me into the schoolroom, the children crowded up, and it was really touching to see how interested they were to see me. Mr. F. drove us out to his home, and the flowers poured in, so that by evening my vases and bouquets covered the piano in the drawing-room at the hotel.

"The negro waiter said, 'Some more of your little cousins here to see you, Misse Haben; lots of relations here, haven't you.' And the other guests at the hotel began to wonder at my fame."

At Jacksonville, Fa., she renewed her cold. On the 19th, she says, "We had our most trying day, when it seemed as if we both should be taken away from the children." They reached Palatka on the 23d, and here began to improve. They afterwards went to Orange Springs, twenty-five miles in the interior.

Feeling much benefited by the journey, they left Florida in April, intending to return slowly overland. Ill news reached them at Washington. It was feared that Louy, the baby, who showed symptoms of lameness, was going to have a "white swelling." Her expression of trust in God's providence, of reliance on the "firm foundation" of His promises in her distress at this intelligence, is very touching. She writes:

> "Reached home with hearts too thankful for words. Found the children good, and much improved. The place looking so pleasant, and but for baby's lameness there would not be a drawback. He is still delicate, and in arms, but has begun to recover."

That summer she commenced a juvenile, "Where There's a Will There's a Way," in which she makes use of her winter's experience, and her Florida material. Business perplexities brought a fearful strain upon her husband's health, which alarmed her very much; but she writes:

"Except that one despairing evening in July, I have nothing with which to reproach myself, so good was God in the extremity, saving me from the temptation to despond and repine, by the simple assurance that He was pledged to help and support us as His children.

"No ray of light, but still helped to rely on that miraculous providence which God is sometimes pleased to exert in our greatest extemity."

"*7th.*

"The peril is averted. I have been happy all day with the thought of God's goodness to us.

"'Fear not I am with thee, oh, be not dismayed,
I, I am thy God, and will still give thee aid;
I'll strengthen thee, help thee, and cause thee to stand,
Upheld by my righteous, omnipotent hand.'"

"*17th.*

"Finished my book. I scarcely realized before in what a month of struggle and despondency it was written."

Brave little heart! Living her philosophy and her religion alike, and so facing unblanched "the lions in the way."

Her fears for her husband were so ever-present, and so absorbing, that she did not become conscious of her own peril. Her life proceeded as before; her domestic cares, her writing—for during the previous winter she had relinquished none of her engagements; her anxieties and exertions for others remained unabated. She went into the city quite frequently, and would often spend a whole day in attending to matters of business for herself or others, returning at night so utterly overcome with fatigue that it was impossible not to feel alarmed for her. But to remonstrances she would reply:

"It is *only* fatigue; I can always sleep it off; I would not do it if there were not always so many things to be done which I can't help feeling that I can do better than any one else; that these tiresome journeys are necessary."

In the autumn, she and her sister made arrangements for their young sister K. to spend a year or two at a boarding-school in Charleston, S. C. K.'s health, and the peculiar advantages of the school, made the place sure to be an admirable one, and "secession" had not yet taken shape, awaiting the result of the presidential election. When the day came for K. to sail, a furious storm was raging, so furious that the ladies of the family in town were questioning whether it would be best to attempt to accompany K. to the ship, which could not possibly sail while the storm lasted, though it might at any moment of its abatement. In the midst of the gale Mrs. Haven made her appearance, having come into town and crossed over to Brooklyn in the height of its fury. "It was impossible to let Katie go without giving her *bon voyage.*"

Of course she accompanied her to the ship, and saw her made comfortable there, and then she returned to her country home; but the exposure at every change from house to carriage was so great, that she was literally drenched. The gale was so terrible that the house itself seemed to rock, the rain burst into it at various places; her dressing closet did not escape, and she even had difficulty in getting dry clothing from any source. One of the noble trees that gave name to the place fell prostrate on the lawn, almost striking the house in its descent; the crash in the gathering darkness of the storm, and the coming of night, frightened the servants and children, and added to the effect the exhaustion and drenching of the day had produced. But

Mrs. Haven's feeling and fears were not the consequences of such fatigues in herself. She writes:

"The violence of this awful storm kept me wakeful, wearied and overtaxed as I was; so I lay on my bed sleepless till nearly morning, praying that God would take care of my poor child on ship-board; toward morning, quite comforted by an inward assurance that all was well with her, I fell asleep."

At another time during that fall, she made her appearance in town so early, that it was evident she had risen before dawn. She said to the person on whom she called:

"I am going over to Philadelphia at two o'clock; but meanwhile I have some little business matters to arrange, will you drive with me for an hour or two?"

When in the carriage the lady was informed that she was to accompany Mrs. Haven to a publishing house, where the former had engaged to have a book published.

"You never do business in a proper way," said Mrs. H., "and though I have every confidence in the gentlemanly publishers, I always make contracts myself, and I am too much interested in this book to allow any informality in the business transaction."

"I never can go upon the supposition that my books are going to be profitable, and that it is worth while to have so much formality."

"I have asked God's blessing upon your work literally, not only that it '*may prosper in the thing whereunto it is sent*,' and be a fountain of good, as it must be, but that it may be successful in a pecuniary point of view, which also we have a *right* to ask."

"I detest business interviews and arrangements."

"What a foolish thing for a sensible woman to say. *I enjoy them*, especially when I can have things my own way! I like to unravel a tangle or open a clear skein; it is as fine as getting out a problem in Algebra, and much more in my line! I like to use what little knowledge of business I have, and exercise my tact if necessary—and I have always very pleasant business interviews. I wrote to Mr. H. the other day that I would go down with you to-day, agreeing to be there at eleven o'clock, and I asked him to have a contract for this book drawn up and ready to sign. It is simply wise and just to do things in this way; a great deal of trouble is prevented, and when that is the case, it is not a question of likes and dislikes."

The contract was signed, and the lady was then requested to make another call with Mrs. Haven. She, Mrs. H., had some years before edited the writings of a deceased friend, and for that, and for writing a preface to the book, had received a sum of money which she had invested for the friend's child, to be used when it should be most needed, "for situated as the little Alice is, there is no knowing how soon the need may come." She had begun to fear that the investment was not a wise one, and her business now was to make some inquiries about it, and to withdraw the money if this seemed best. Thus the morning was spent, as were many others of this singularly useful life.

On New Year's night, 1861, Mrs. Haven writes:

"Alone for the first time on my wedding-day. I cannot let it pass without a record of the unlooked for experience I am passing through.

"S. coughing badly decides to try Santa Cruz for the winter. I had not the least idea of going with him, for badly as he coughs, and nervously shattered as he is, he is far more comfortable than he was last year at this time. But on my return from Philadelphia, where I had gone for a week, he asked me to get ready to go away with him at Christmas. There were all kinds of arrangements to be made, in the midst of which, becoming uneasy about himself, he went off *via* Havana, by steamer, leaving me to follow in a sailing vessel. The friends upon whom he depended to accompany me are not going, so I expect to start alone on the 5th, in a brig bound for St. Thomas. *Alone to-day too*—I rest upon the promise, 'In quietness and confidence shall be your strength;' but sometimes I shrink from the loneliness, the parting with the children, the dangers of the sea, so peculiarly dreaded by me, and above all lest I have been rash or self-willed in my ideas of duty.

"I have abundant blessings to be thankful for in the year past. When I remember how extremely ill S. was a year ago to-day, his wonderful restoration, my own comparative health, the improvement in Louy, the health of the others, and all other known, and many more unknown mercies, I heartily bless and thank God."

"Alone" she went on, in the little sailing vessel, the "Addy Swift;" and after a voyage in which she suffered much less than she expected, she reached St. Thomas, when she felt fully compensated for all her anxieties and alarms by finding her husband, from whom she had not heard since his leaving for Havana, in the little boat which pulled out to meet them, as they dropped anchor in the beautiful bay.

They passed a little while at this island, and then went on to St. Croix, where they soon found themselves comfortably established in a fine house at the West End, or Frederickstadt. Theodore Parker had boarded at this same house the year before, and in his recently-published memoir, are graphic descriptions of this beautiful island, and of the family where the Havens now found a resting-place.

On presenting letters to the rector of the English church, the Rev. Mr. Dubois, Mrs. Haven's name was instantly recognized, and she was told that her little books were in the Sunday School library, and very much esteemed, so that even here in this remote place her good name had gone before her, and prepared a welcome for her.

She enjoyed her sojourn at Frederickstadt very much, especially their rambles on the beach, and their horseback rides over the island. Her graphic letters to her friends were delightful. She wrote much, and even exerted herself, when not fit to make such exertion, to write an article for Mr. Godey. An attack of ophthalmia, the result, she says, of the unmitigated sunshine, interrupted this writing; but she resumed it as soon as possible, and esteemed herself fortunate in an opportunity to send off the manuscript and a package of letters, by a vessel bound directly to the United States, which had touched at the island. This package, prepared with so much pains, never reached its destination, the vessel being wrecked at sea.

Another disappointment which she felt very much, might as well be mentioned here. The history of the island interested her extremely. She took every opportunity to procure information about certain interesting epochs in its history, especially all that related to the emancipation of the negroes, and its effect socially, and on the commercial prosperity of the island.

The preparation of this sketch for publication was the last important piece of writing which she did, and was made when she was so feeble that the labor was probably the finishing stroke, being the immediate cause of her fearful illness in the following winter. The paper required illustrations, which had been prepared for it by an artist who was at Santa Cruz with them. A disagreement between this gentleman and the publishers caused the delay of its publication, and finally prevented it altogether. This added to the peculiar fatality which seemed to attend all her literary labor at the island.

After some weeks, during which they had had no news from home, the travellers returned to this country. In the interval the most startling events had occurred, and they landed in New York just as the people were in the ferment following the fall of Sumter, and in the midst of the preparations for the war which now devastates our land.

Mrs. Haven says the contrast to the land and life they had left cannot be described. At first she could not comprehend or appreciate the excitement she encountered, but before a week had elapsed she writes:

"I watched our fine Seventh Regiment passing down Broadway, on its way to Washington, with feelings so keenly alive to 'the situation,' that I fairly would have felt it a relief to join in the expressions of enthusiasm to which the immense crowd constantly gave voice in cheers and hurrahs. I find myself quite a patriotic American again, and am glad to be in my own land."

## CHAPTER V.

*THE SUMMER OF* 1861.

S the war cloud gathered blackness, the intense interest of Mrs. Haven in the condition of the country was manifested in every way. No one was more active than she in those movements in which a woman could engage; and when her hands could do no more, her heart was always brimming with the fulness of emotion aroused by the suffering on the battle-field, and in the desolate households to which ill-tidings came from time to time.

When the battle of Bull Run was being fought, she was moved as only those of fine and unnaturally quickened spiritual apprehensions are, while a great event is pulling the heart strings of a nation. The news which reached them on Sunday was hopeful, but during Monday, before the knowledge of the fatal result could reach her, she says:

"I was possessed by such a spirit of restlessness, that it was entirely impossible for me to remain quiet, or to occupy myself with any thing sufficiently absorbing to keep my thoughts away from the battle-field. I spent hours praying for the dying and the bereaved; and whether in the house, or walking about the grounds, or sitting on the piazza with closed eyes, my heart went up continually in petition to the God of battles and to the Father of Mercies."

As the afternooon trains from the city began to arrive, she walked down the carriage road to the gate that she might get the intelligence she craved. A person who saw her standing there at the foot of the avenue was struck by her appearance, and described her as one who seemed consumed by a fever—a purple flame in her cheeks and a glittering fire in her eyes, which were softened by tears as the story of the disaster was told.

When she knew all that was to be related of that pitiful fight and sorry flight, she returned quickly to the house and shut herself up in her room, where she alternately prayed and wrote. The feeling that found utterance in such circumstances was a poem called "Bull Run," which appeared in many of the leading papers of the day, but may have escaped some eyes; the heart that conceived it throbs in every line:

### BULL RUN, SUNDAY, JULY 21st.

BY ALICE B. HAVEN.

We—walking so slowly adown the green lane,
With sabbath-bells chiming, and birds singing psalms,
He—eager with haste, pressing on o'er the slain,
'Mid the trampling of steeds and the drum-beat to arms;
In that cool dewy morning.

We—waiting with faces all reverent and still,
The organ's voice vibrant with praise unto God.
His face set like flint with the impress of will,
To press back the foe, or to die on the sod—
My fair, brave young brother'

We—kneeling to hear benedictions of love,
Our hearts all at peace with the message from Heaven!
He—stretched on the field, gasping, wounded to prove
If mercy were found where such courage had thriven,
In the midst of the slaughter.

Oh, God!—can I live with the horrible truth!
Stabbed through as he lay, with their glittering steel,
Could they look in that face, like a woman's for youth,
And crush out its beauty with musket and heel,
Like hounds, or like demons!

That brow I have blessed in my dead mother's place,
 Each morning and eve since she went unto rest;
Smoothing down the fair cheek, as my own baby's face,
 Those eyes with her look, where my kisses were prest,
  For I saw hers—so tender!

Curses spring to my lips! Oh, my God, send the hail
 Of swift, ready vengeance for deeds such as this!
Forego all Thy mercy, if judgment must fail!
 Forgive my wild heart if it prayeth amiss—
  His blood crieth upward.

"Amiss!"—and the strife of my clamorous grief
 Is hushed into stillness,—what grief like to thine!
If my poor human heart with its passions so brief
 Is tortured with pangs can we guess the Divine,
  With depths past all searching?

I know eyes more tender looked upward to Thee,
 That visage so marred by the torturing crown—
Those smooth, noble limbs racked with anguish I see;
 The side where the blood and the water gushed down
  From stroke fierce and brutal.

Help lips white with anguish take up his prayer;
 Help hearts that are bursting to stifle their cries,
The shout of the populace, too, has been there,
 To drown pleas for justice, to clothe truth in lies—
  To enrage and to madden.

They knew not we loved them; they knew not we prayed
 For their weal as our own: "we are brethren," we plead—
Unceasing those prayers to our Father were made:
 When they flung down the palm for palmetto we said,
  "Let us still hope to win them."

"God so loved that He gave!" We are giving to these
The lives that were dearer to us than our own—
Let us add prayer for blow, trusting God to appease
Our hearts' craving pain, when He hears on His throne
"Oh, Father, forgive them!"

There are few records of importance during this summer. Her health was not very good, and, provided with a pretty set of garden tools, she spent much time out of doors. She wrote less also, but she was not willing to confess to invalidism, nor was her daily routine essentially changed. She was always "a little tired," and always looking forward to some time when she should feel rested again. Alas! for the poor weary body. When could rest come to it, while the warm, loving heart beat, and the eager, unselfish spirit stirred within it!

In one letter she says:

"I lie down and rise up with the desolation of the widow and the childless encompassing me. I pray always that God will give wisdom to our rulers, and bring peace to this poor land."

In another, to her sister, "Mary E.":

"*My work is done.* I have this morning finished 'The Good Report,' and I come to you to be congratulated. I have left it to you to revise in case I should not live to do it. There is little to be done but to copy and to transpose some paragraphs which are marked. You know how long I have been at it, ever since the Cottage days—four years at least; and if it never sees print, I feel fully repaid for the work, by all it has taught me. Perhaps this is all it ever will accomplish."

On September 13th, in her journal:

"I have a birthday blessing to ask for S., that he may be delivered from all 'blindness of heart;' the same for myself; but above all that I may conquer *sloth*, my present besetting sin, the sin of the year, *my* sin of prosperity.

"This is the answer to my prayer in my regular reading:

"'*For thou shalt drive out the Canaanites though they have iron chariots, and be strong.*'

"Here are besetting sins described:

"'*Yet the children of Manasseh could not drive out the inhabitants of those cities, but the Canaanites would dwell in the land.*'

"'*Yet it came to pass when the children of Israel were waxen strong, that they put the Canaanites to tribute, but did not utterly drive them out.*'

"So we rest content with putting limits on our own faults, but do not utterly conquer them. '*The slothful soul must tarry there longer.*' Lord grant me grace to discover, to avoid, to resist, and to cast out whatever is evil within me. And here is the prayer for help for daily renewed assistance in the lesson of my morning reading on my birthday:

"'*Give me a blessing, for thou hast given me a south land*' (a desire to do right and a knowledge of my duty). '*Give me also springs* of water.'"

After an enumeration of all the blessings of the year, she closes with:

"Then, too, I am relieved from my nervous headaches, from which I have suffered, with little respite, for fifteen years. Last winter appears to have cured them entirely. Altogether this has been one of the happiest summers of my life, in my own family and home, and never were happiness and prosperity more undeserved."

As Thanksgiving Day of 1861 drew near, her heart, in its wide identification with the stricken and the suffering, poured itself out in a poem, which she called

### "IN THE FIRES." *

THANKSGIVING DAY, 1861.

Husband and child are not, we turn and falter,
  To-day our hearts with anguished memories swell;
How can *we* bring thanks-offerings to Thine altar,
  Who scarce have learned to say, "My God 'tis well"?

Thanks we were chosen? Marked for cruel scourging.
  Thanks for the pangs that wring us yet? The pain
Of parting, prayers unheard for all their urging,
  The awful dread—*their names told with the dead!*

* "*Wherefore glorify ye the Lord in the fires.*"

Last year we counted them by tender kisses,
  Thanked Thee with tears for each dear loving face;
That Thou hast answered even voiceless wishes,
  And now—an empty—echoing, household place!

One year, but *one*, and all this desolation!
  Bidden *a song* from out its depths to raise!
Sackcloth and ashes gird a stricken nation,
  We cannot cast them off for hymns of praise.

The widowed wife, the yearning, childless mother,
  How can *they* kneel, and say, "*I thank Thee Lord*"?
Leave them, pass by them, ask it of some other
  Who counts untouched to-day, the heart's fond hoard.

But *faith* takes up and stills such wild desires,
  And God be thanked for those who yet can stand
*To glorify Him even in the fires*,
  The martyr fires that light and try the land.

Another poem must find place here which she never gave to the public. When the news came of the burning of Charleston, her heart remembered the dear friends whose beautiful homes had opened hospitably to her, and her young sister still abiding in the fated city; but the significance of the terrible judgment could not be put aside by tender memories, and she wrote:

OUR ALAS!

God is not slack concerning words of promise,
  As men count slackness—His "I will repay,"
Though spoken low, so low we failed to hear it,
  We find fulfilled before our eyes to-day.

Oh sister city! lifting thy tall spires,
  Unconscious of the strange avenging fate!
Brought from this height to sit in dust and ashes,
  In one short hour cast down and desolate!

How quickly had we come thy need to succor,
  Quickly unfurled the white wings of our sails,
Freighted them with our best, our chiefest treasure,
  And prayed the while for fair and favoring gales.

But thine own will repelled and cast us from thee,
  Severed the bonds that linked our lives with thine,
Bared thy proud head to storms that might assault thee,
  Defied all law, the human, the Divine.

Compelled, we "stand afar to watch thy burning,"
  With our alas! alas! for thy disdain,
Raising our useless, helpless hands to Heaven,
  While *God sets on thy brow the brand of Cain.*

With her usual earnest interest in every thing she could help or forward, Mrs. Haven had urged her sister to complete a book which had been begun some years before, and thrown aside in consequence of the ill-health of the writer. Having procured a few of the chapters without letting her purpose be known, she had carried them to a publisher, and obtained from him a proposition to publish the work. She then told her sister what was done, and left her no course to pursue but to finish the writing and have it ready in season. So much had been done by Mrs. Haven, and it was so entirely owing to her that the last impulse as well as the first inspiration had been given, that her sister desired to dedicate it to her, and asked permission to do so, accompanying the request with a copy of the dedication she wished to use. It was in these words; and to the sister who had so long, so anxiously, and at last so admiringly watched the course and growth in character of Alice Haven, nothing less seemed just:

"My Dear Sister:

"I owe it to your example and sympathy that I have found courage, under the burden of feeble health and exacting home cares, to finish this little book.

"You have been the best example to me of the lessons I strive to teach; and you have best shown me how *certainly*, by the grace of God, *the victory is given* to such as struggle in humble patience, and in self-abnegation, with the infirmities of our nature.

"May I not then dedicate to you these pages, in which

I would point others to the heights all may reach, who lay down self to serve God and bless the world?

"I am sure you will add to mine, your prayers that the blessing of God, which you have never sought in vain upon your work, may rest on mine.

"With respect and love born of our tender relationship, and nourished to maturity by this mutual service,

"I am always your loving sister,

"C. H. B. R."

This answer was returned:

"And now I must say how much your dedication surprised and touched me; but, dear sister, if I suffer myself to listen to the 'well done' here, I shall miss it hereafter. You know it is my greatest temptation. I cannot think that it is right to let it go out. S. will like it from you, but whether he will like to have it printed I cannot tell. I think not."

To a long plea for its publication, made by her sister in her next letter, she replied:

"I do not undervalue commendation, far from it. Sometimes you have written words of appreciation that have cheered, and comforted, and helped me, as nothing else could. We all like to know that some one we trust appreciates us; it helps us to put up with the indifference and undervaluation of every-day people. Sometimes when I have felt myself misunderstood and unappreciated by some connected with me, by those around me, when this has pressed heavily, I have felt that there was *One who did know* my struggle to help and uphold those to whom I refer, and who have seemed ready '*to turn again and rend me*'—how I have borne with them, and tried to make them happy. It has taught me '*to do it as unto the Lord,*' and to leave all my doings unto '*my Father which seeth in secret*' for reward, not even seeking, or rather not depending upon a recognition of effort by those for whom it was made. One does look for it unconsciously, but it does not hurt me as it used to, when I don't find it; and again, when I do, from you especially, I feel 'God sends it,' and so it is doubly sweet.

"You say you praise me because I have overcome faults. I never work against faults of character. I *strive against sins, that* is the overcoming with me. I learned to get up in season that we might have prayers before S. went to town, because I knew it was wrong to neglect them. I tried to check a tendency to exaggeration, not because it was a blemish, but an untruth; so of irritability and all the rest of the train.

"Don't think your dedication did not touch and please me. It only seemed *so much too high praise;* and of course if written by a sister I must know of it, and sanction it; while if a friend had done it, people could not say 'how egotistical,' or 'mutual admiration,' or any of those things which they like to charge against literary people; and I could not bear to have any thing meant so truly and tenderly, subjected to ill-natured remarks. You must understand me just as I mean, that I strive so hard for humility, and not to think of myself more highly than I ought to think, that this seems to set me, as we once said, 'at the top of the ladder, instead of the foot of the Cross.'

"You know if people compliment you on certain things that you set no value on, you are not in the least moved if the praise is ever so glowing; but if they touch certain other points, things you *do* aspire to, it reaches you. So it is with me; all my ambition and endeavour being set this way, to be called 'good' is more to me than all that could be said in any other form of praise. Therefore I am afraid of it.

"I don't believe now, that I have made you comprehend me. I am afraid you will think me cold, when you have paid me the highest and tenderest tribute one mother's child could pay another; but you asked me to talk about it, and pen and ink are so slow and blundering."

The dedication was used notwithstanding this protest, though after the publication of the book, Mrs. Haven felt it even more than she thought, and never loaned or gave away a copy of "Springs of Action," without an apology for the personality.

In the success of this work, and all others that her sister had written, and especially in the literary success of her young sister-in-law, Mary E. Bradley, whose ventures as an authoress appeared from time to time, Mrs. Haven was keenly interested. Her suggestions were wise in regard to the execution of a book, and its publication. Even to her brother-in-law, after his long intimacy with the book-world, her suggestions were often valuable.

She kept herself informed of the condition of the book market, understood and used her tact for the benefit of all in whom she was interested, *which was all whom she could serve.*

Not infrequently foreign books were submitted to her judgment by publishers who were not certain of their value for republication. In her quiet country home there was always a fresh book atmosphere, a consciousness to the guest that intellectual needs could be satisfied, and stimulus found. She says of an occasional visitor, who was peculiarly able to minister to this attraction of "The Willows":

"It is delightful to get a fresh breeze from the literary world, as I always do with M. I cannot take much of it, because I find it exciting and stimulating beyond what I am able to bear now. His short visits, with his good music, and his rich, fresh nature and knowledge, bring me great pleasure. At first, I grew restless sometimes when it forced upon me the contrast between my old life and this, so dull to the superficial observer; but I soon return to a healthful appreciation of the blessedness of my lot. I know you always wonder at my content so 'far from the spot in the lake where the stone drops in,' as Mrs. S. says. You do not realize what this life has done for me, how it has been God's greatest blessing, for which I never can be thankful enough."

There are some who dread, and who complain of stagnation in slow currents, or the quiet pool. Stagnation was impossible to one in whose soul living waters were pouring out their sweetness; to one whose great, warm heart was always ready to nourish a brain too active and creative to suffer from depletion in the keenest excitement, or stagnation in the dullest routine.

## CHAPTER VI.

### *HER FIRST ILLNESS.*

THE delicate health of Mrs. Haven saw no improvement during 1861. At first, as we have seen, she struggled against her weariness, considering it simply a disinclination to exertion, now that the pressure of past years was taken off. She had seen some whom she had been educating become self-supporting, and many whom she had assisted pecuniarily, placed in more favorable circumstances. Mr. Haven was prosperous in business, and new channels did not open before her as formerly; she could not but feel that God was requiring less of her.

A peculiar disposition of her leisure now occurred to her. She wrote letters to all in whom she was especially interested, to every person for whose welfare she had ever had a feeling of responsibility. She did not speak of this at the time, but it came to light in various ways before a twelve-month had passed. After she had become too ill to attend to her letters, and even after she had left the country, some of these letters found their way back which had been sent by her to her old Sunday School pupils in Philadelphia, from the "Dead Letter" office. Children, who had now become men and women, were startled by a word from their former teacher, or through their change of residence failed to receive the affectionate appeals she sent to them. She wrote to, or sought out every person who had ever been in her employ, or whom she had befriended, and could still reach. Once afterwards, she said of this impulse:

"I do not know what impelled me; partly, perhaps, an unacknowledged consciousness that my life was drawing to a close; partly that having more leisure I went back to the old channels."

It must be remarked that these were not the

first letters written to her old Sunday School pupils. Amongst her papers were found many letters written to her year after year, in reply to hers addressed to them; what these had been the letters in reply bore witness to. There were also letters from many others who looked to her as their guide in spiritual things. Some wrote regularly once a year, frequently at Christmas times, bringing their offering of grateful affection, their unfailing acknowledgment of her tender care and faithfulness. Neither time, nor distance, nor change of circumstance, ever sufficed to efface her interest in these, or to relieve her of her sense of responsibility for influence, or the means to aid others.

In one case a lad who had been led to Christ by the reading of one of her Sunday School books, encouraged by her, devoted himself to the Christian ministry. She took the most affectionate interest in her 'godson,' as she used to style him, and his Christmas offering was always welcomed with more than common thankfulness by her. As a clergyman of the Episcopal Church, he is now bringing in the sheaves from her sowing, as do many others in other callings, who have been taught by her to sanctify their gifts to the service of the Master.

During the autumn of 1861 one cold followed another; she had restless, feverish days and nights, and finally plueritic symptoms. The idea of danger to herself had now to be sometimes admitted; but then she still seemed to have so much to do, and her life-work had been so blessed in its doing, that she was most reluctant to believe it could be closing. Her references in her letters to her health were always such as could relieve the fears of her friends, and encourage them to believe that she suffered little. She spoke of it seldom, and slightly, and often in a vein of humor, as if she was magnifying the ill; but those who knew her, even those who read her cheerful letters, were not deceived. The hollow cheek with its bright hectic, the languid eye, and drooping lid, and bent shoulders were unerring indications of her condition.

To "Mary E." she wrote in January, 1862:

"I thank you very much for your note, which I cannot pretend to answer. I am afraid of my pen, but I mean to live to take my revenge on it for getting me into so much trouble. I have been preparing for this cold for a long time, and only fear I was too well prepared for it! I think it is breaking up for good. The pleuritic pain, which was the worst of all, is gone. I told mother to tell you that I did not think any one fully appreciated my danger but you. When you are determined on being 'dangerous' if any body tells you 'you don't look ill, Mrs. H,' or 'not half as ill as I expected,' it's very irritating indeed, and a great relief to have one sympathetic friend think there's something in it. S. won't let me stir out, or write a line if he knows it; and only think of S. P. and the G.'s, and everybody else in town, who won't came again for a year! I have been babyish enough to feel the disappointment.

"Only think of the selfish happiness of thinking people would miss you if you really did die! It was quite a new idea, and I hugged it! I really looked for your note. I knew *you'd* be sorry."

At last news came to those who loved her, that Alice Haven was prostrated by a fearful hemorrhage; and to all who knew of her devoted life, and especially to the few who had come to know the care with which she seemed to be settling all those affairs to which she had given such anxious thought, this illness was thought to be death's harbinger indeed. But she can best tell the story. She lived through the peril of the attack, and on the 13th of September, 1862, we find another birthday record:

"My thirty-fifth birthday! 'Half way home,' even at the longest, and, as it would seem, much nearer in reality.

"I have a record of watchful care and kindness to make. The sloth which I grieved over a year ago to-day, was in some respects *not* a fault, as I look back upon it; and though cheerful and joyful even, all the autumn and during the early part of the winter, I was tired and very feverish, with a constant slight cough, rattling respiration, and a slight sore throat.

"Dr. P. made light of it, and I paid little attention to it myself till after Christmas. Louy was very ill from Christmas till New Year's Day. I took a heavy cold about the same time, and had a cough and hectic fever every night. Up to January 1st I wrote regularly (besides often assisting in some household duties), to finish up in advance six months of my work on the Lady's Book, little thinking it was my last! I intended then to commence rewriting 'The Good Report,' which I had finished in August. The first two weeks of the New Year, I hurried to prepare an article for 'Harper,' on St. Croix, which after all they have not used, though it was the last stroke in bringing on my illness. In fact it was all written in pain and exhaustion."

"*Jan. 29th.*

"I had a severe attack of pleurisy, and suffered much, my cough growing deeper and deeper. I began to make arrangements for going to town for change of air and scene. S. proposed that I should visit a friend in Thirty-ninth Street instead of going to a hotel, as was our first intention.

"I consulted Dr. G. first, who told me that I was threatened with 'old-fashioned consumption,' and must use great care, that my left lung was already affected. On February 13th, after having made unusual exertion to talk the evening before to a gentleman who was partially deaf, I sat reading my morning lesson, when the words: '*This sickness is not unto death*,' came into my mind. For a time I did not associate any idea with them, but they returned so persistently that I turned to chapter and verse and read them. A moment or two after I found that I was raising blood for the first time. Alarmed at first, the text was at once a promise and comfort that never left me."

The day before this occurred Mrs. Haven had driven out, and knowing that a friend was in deep sorrow, had paid her a visit. She was asked up-stairs to the lady's own room. She said, for a moment, she thought it impossible to go up those two flights of stairs, but the hope of being able to say a comforting word was so strong, that she toiled up to the third story, though almost too much exhausted to speak when she entered the room.

The journal goes on:

"I had risen and dressed on Saturday, and was making my way to the library, for I remembered some writing which must be done, indeed I had been occupied part of the week in getting material for the expected article. I managed to supply the opening pages, when a hemorrhage came on, and I laid down my pen for a napkin, which a servant brought me. I had done my last work of that kind!

"The hemorrhage lasted from twelve till five, with intervals of rest. S. came in just at the last and helped me to bed. He said as he opened the hall door he heard me cough, and knew by the gurgling sound accompanying it what was going on. My friend was exceedingly kind, doing all that a sister could have done. I regretted extremely the unforeseen care and exertion that thus came upon her. During the night I made up my mind that it was a violent attack of pneumonia, relieved by the hemorrhage, and that I should get perfectly well again; but Dr. Parker said distinctly the next day that there were tubercles on the right lung, and that I must think of, and care for myself as an invalid.

"The prospect of death in that extreme exhaustion would not have been so hard to bear, as this doom to the weary, care-worn life of an invalid, wandering about for health; pitied, discussed as such, *shut out from active employment.* It was what I had never looked forward to for myself, and for a time my courage and faith entirely failed me. I knew I had deserved this. I had even talked lightly of the possibility of my death with Mr. H. and others. I knew being allowed to give way thus, was a punishment."

A few days after she said to her sister, who had come to her as soon as she heard of her illness:

"I think I was punished for another thing. I really think I had done one of the most *faithless* deeds of my life. I was growing covetous, grasping, and was unmindful of the promises I have leaned on so many years, which have never failed me."

Then after an interval, indeed all this was said very slowly, and almost in a whisper:

"I had begun to think that perhaps God was giving us now what he meant us to put aside, as you know I have never done for the children or myself, something for the future. S. has his capital in his business. Some day it might be lost again, as before. So this winter I began *my* saving, putting into bank three hundred dollars, a beginning toward a sum to be expended in the education of the children. As soon as I did this, God took my work out of my hands. It was not the way he wished me to use what I have always felt to be money entrusted to me for His service; and you know, sister, till this temptation came it has been spent so unreservedly, and thus I was shown my error. If I can ever work again, how faithfully will I do *His* work; and I *may*, for I know '*this sickness is not unto death.*'"

The listener to these broken and faintly-uttered words, looked at the fragile being before her, and at the transparent little hand that for so many years had wrought so nobly in His service, and felt that this condemnation of self could not be merited, would never have come to a mind and conscience less tender and true, and full of love of the service which had occupied the best years of her life, and many, manv hours of pain and weakness.

Her journal continues:

"While I lay there so helpless, and wishing they would 'let me go down,' and not make me struggle for life, S. was called from the room. They were afraid to tell me that Katie had come from Charleston; but *I knew it must be so*, and *that* great anxiety was at an end. She had been brought safely through the horrors of war, under the last flag of truce that was allowed for many months. She was here to remain at 'The Willows' with our mother and the children, in case we went away again, as was possible if I recovered enough to go.

"The way was thus open to me, and my path was made clear. I felt as I had never done before, that I should never again doubt God's guidance and tenderness. But I shall, a thousand times, if I live long enough!

"I was so weak at first that I could not rise in bed. Every one was very kind and attentive. By Wednesday sister came, and the next Saturday I saw mother and the children; poor little things, they little knew what threatened them!

"The plans for our going away ended in our taking passage for Nassau, in the steamer of March 1st. I gained steadily and rapidly, and was able to be carried out home for a day or two. On the 1st I was brought in town to stay at a hotel till the steamer sailed. '*Goodness and mercy followed me*' from first to last. Sister was with me, and many friends called."

An incident may be mentioned showing the care and attention to her comfort and her wishes which awaited her all the time, and causes such grateful acknowledgments. The friend whose visits to "The Willows," and whose singing of sacred music gave her such especial pleasure, was living at this hotel. She had said, speaking of her loneliness on the previous Sunday evening: "How much I wished as I was lying up-stairs in my room, that M. would come and play and sing for me. The music of 'Oh cast thy burden on the Lord,' with its sweeter meaning, floated through my mind all the evening."

This was mentioned to the gentleman. When he found that a room had been engaged at the hotel for Mrs. Haven, he made an effort at once to get a larger and more quiet room than could be had at the time of the engagement. Into this he placed a piano; and when she was brought in and saw the ample room with its glowing fire, luxurious couch and easy chairs, all the result of his thoughtfulness, fresh flowers, new books and open piano, she said, looking about in astonishment, "What Prima Donna has just gone away?"

During the three or four days which they had to wait for the sailing of the Karnak, which was waiting for European mails, her health continued to improve. She was able to see her friends, and to enjoy their conversation, though she could not take much part in it. She was refreshed with the music she had coveted whenever she was able to listen to it, and she never wearied of the sweet "sentence" which had comforted her that Sunday evening. The tears trickled through her thin fingers as she lay on the couch, in her usual attitude, with her hand over her eyes; but her heart was filled and *satisfied* with the consciousness that "goodness and mercy followed her from first to last."

"What a precious Sabbath!" she said, as the music ceased, and she had listened to the reading of a favorite chapter, "I have worshipped, 'giving thanks' all day long."

She was supported from her room to the carriage, and so to the ship, but she was already making rapid strides toward a recovery.

In her *first* letter from Nassau, to her sister, she writes:

> "I have walked a mile, and can do any number of stairs. When you recall me as you saw me last, this will seem incredible; but the voyage and the climate have done wonders. I have yet reached no greater weight than eighty-four pounds."

At Nassau she wrote the verses recently published for the first time, written for a friend there, for they found the place full of invalids:

### IN THE VALLEY.

Gently sloped the rugged pathway
  To her fainting, failing tread,
Downward to the dreary valley
  By her Saviour gently led.
Day by day she neared the darkness,
  Leaning on that steadfast arm;
As a child who fears no danger,
  Shrinks not from approaching harm;
Till she walked within the shadow,
  Little dreaming where she trod,
Knowing not, the "staff" sustaining,
  That she passed beneath the "rod;"
Knowing not how short the distance
  To the home she longed to see;
Thinking in the far-off future
  There were terrors yet to be.

For the love in which she trusted,
  Upward drew her waiting eyes;
Till we saw them change and brighten
  With a smile of glad surprise.
She had guessed not of the darkness,
  Till she saw the breaking day,
Caught no glimpse of death's dark shadows
  Till they changed and fled away.
Gentle life, with gentlest closing,
  Could we wish for aught more blest,
Could we ask more sweet transition
  To the promised land of rest?

As the editor of the Lady's Book says: "It

depicts so truthfully her own future, that it seems like a whispering from the angels of her own 'transition to the land of rest.'"

Their time at Nassau passed very pleasantly, except the drawback of a little depression in consequence of the suffering, in some cases so helpless which they saw about them. Some of their letters to residents of the island had been sent them by an aged lady, the widow of a former official there. She paid Mrs. Haven the graceful compliment of sending to each person to whom she gave her a letter, a copy of one of her own books!

They expected to return in the Karnak; but while watching her enter the harbor, on her way back from Havana, the steamer struck on a rock, and went down in their sight. They therefore were compelled, she says, "to set sail in a crowded vessel, 'The Alma,' and had a dull, comfortless voyage of ten days; but I returned *so well, without even a lingering cough.* I continued so up to this month (September), *wonderfully well*, and able to accomplish all usual social and domestic duties."

## CHAPTER VII.

*AN INTERVAL OF HEALTH.*

IN the summer of 1862 Mrs. Haven seemed to regain something of the old poise. She was careful of over-exertion, after the serious warning of the year before, and she never returned to her old habits of writing. Only after long intervals, and then for a short period, would she venture to use her pen. Of this enforced state of things, the consequence of severe compulsion and sense of duty, she says:

"The hardest trial growing out of my illness has been to obey the advice of my physicians, both Dr. Grey and Dr. Parker, and lay aside my pen. After sixteen years of constant professional occupation, it was a struggle no human friend can appreciate to give up my business engagements.

"With regard to being relieved from the long drudgery of my work, this was from the first constantly in my mind, *for I saw God's own hand in the clear signature of the release, 'I eased his shoulders from the burden, and his hands were delivered from making the pots.'*"

Some disappointments attended what had been natural expectations, when she gave up her engagements, one of which particularly gave her great pain. She writes:

"I depend too much upon appreciation. This was to show me that I must remain satisfied with waiting for the 'well done' hereafter. It was a blessing in disguise, that the choice of a return to my work was not given to me, as I never should have thought it right to *give up* the occupation at all, from the belief that all that I could earn (when spent conscientiously for others, as I had opportunity) was a duty. Therefore, it was clearly taken out of my hands. As I should have hesitated about taking it up again, no choice was allowed me.

"Yet at the time this was most painful; the uncertainty about the future of some very dear to me, the finding other channels for employment, and being thrown so entirely from the old activity.

"S. would say, 'Why do you grieve over it? You have long worried because you wanted more time for your children, or your studies, or social duties. Now it is given, why do you fret?'

"In one of these depressed hours I came upon this, which was at the moment, and has been since, the greatest comfort: 'Waste not your time in fears and thoughts of the future, in this world. *To you the future may be short. The things you most fear will probably never disturb you.* If evils come, they will probably be such as no foresight of man can anticipate. '*Trust in the Lord and do good; so shalt thou dwell in the land, and verily thou shall be fed. Delight thyself also in the Lord, and He shall give thee the desire of thy heart.*' "

In the August of this summer she was persuaded to accompany her brother-in-law, and some other friends, to Niagara: "I have so many uses for money, there are so many who need what it would cost to take a pleasure trip, that I never have a sense of ease and enjoyment in spending it on myself," had been one of her objections to the journey; another was her unwillingness to be absent from home over Sunday, the day when her husband was at leisure, and she knew she had it in her power to contribute much to his happiness. This, during all her married life, had been a constantly-urged objection to her making long visits or journeys when he did not accompany her. Her visits to Philadelphia, to her mother or sister, had always been within a week's limit, if possible, for this reason: "You don't realize how much I am needed on Sundays. I could not be happy myself, knowing how he was missing me," she would say.

All objections overcome through the urgency of those who wished her to have the pleasure, once so singularly, and since then, so indefinitely deferred, she went up to Hudson, where she spent a few days, leaving her oldest child and her oldest nephew, who was spending the summer vacation with her, in the care of some relations, and then proceeded to join the party, who were *en route* at Albany. Her enjoyment of the journey was extreme and perfect. All were surprised at the exertion she was able to make in their excursions at the Falls, walking and even climbing almost as well as the best. She wrote to her sister:

"It was an unclouded visit. The weather, health, and I think everybody's temper and spirits were all we could wish. I have not seen W. so buoyant, so like his old self for many a day. That alone would have been enjoyment for me. It made me think of our old childish Claverack Falls' trips. Can you remember so long ago?

"As for Niagara, it was lovelier and grander than ever I had imagined or expected. I am only sorry that I can never see it again *for the first time.* Every point was finer than the last. The two grandest views to me were from under the cliff on the Canada side, and from the tower on the American. I can easily understand your awe on seeing it as you did at midnight, and with rising clouds at intervals obscuring the moonlight, while a storm wind raged around the tower, for in the broad day light, and familiar with the scene, I was really a coward, standing on that balcony. The force and persistence of the steady fall impressed me most, and the ages in which that chasm had been forming, sawn back into the solid rock.

"You see I have not much to say. I had *nothing* to say then."

To a friend who was with them, she said a few days before her death, "It was the most perfect pleasure trip I ever took;" indeed her enjoyment was as complete as every pulse throbbing with delight could make it.

There was one period of her life when pleasure seemed to pall on her taste, when she turned with indifference, if not disgust, from every thing which did not offer the zestful flavor of a duty performed or a service rendered. Her satisfaction in this journey, and indeed in all the recreation she allowed herself in these later years, was as hearty and complete as in the childish days to which she refers. Her confidence in the Divine guidance, so invariably sought by her, gave her the simple perfect happiness of a child, trusting still in the leading of a Father's hand.

It was during this summer that she occupied herself in the hospital work, out of which grew a story for Harper, which made a great impression at the time of its publication. Many a tender and brave heart was stirred up by it "to go and do likewise," and scores of soldiers wrote to her and to the publishers thanking them for it, and invoking blessings on the hand that penned it. Nothing that she ever wrote brought her a richer and quicker reward of the sort which best repaid her for her exertion. The sketch was called "One Day," and was published in the October Harper, 1862. She was so liberally paid for this story by the courteous publishers, that she found herself able from the proceeds to publish a little *tract* which she wrote, called "In the Hospitals," a simple, sweet appeal, written as she talked, which has gone home to many a soldier's heart, carrying conviction and comfort alike.

A hospital had been erected on David's Island, near New Rochelle, and about five miles from Mrs. Haven's home. To this place she went twice a week in company with some other benevolent ladies, each carrying a basket stored with delicate viands for the sick and wounded, and she bearing to all, such "words in season" as were never wanting from her lips. The long drive, and the exertion during the heat of summer, became after some two months too much for her delicate health, and she had to relinquish the personal service; but she continued to prepare her baskets of delicacies, and when her lips could no longer speak to them, she employed her pen as we have seen.

Of this, and of every good word and work with which her life was crowded, there is no record in her journal. The knowledge has come to us by the testimony of those who shared this service with her, and from the many served during all her life of love and labor; but this testimony has been abundant, so much so that were the limits of this record enlarged, and were not many of the tributes from those she benefited too delicate and personal in their character for publication, a second volume could be prepared with its history of "this deedful life."

In only one letter can there be found a reference to what she had *done*. This was called out by a remark which seemed to attribute selfishness to her in seeking to withdraw from interference in a matter painfully agitated between some whom she loved. Her sympathy only had been sought in the case, but she could never give that alone when she saw any thing else that she could do; and this active sympathy was too much for her strength. It was no selfish feeling, however, that had prompted the wise counsel she here repeats with its reference to her own experience and practice. That it might possibly, even by those who knew and loved her most tenderly, be attributed to such a trait, for *she* saw less unselfishness in herself than others could possibly allow in their estimate of her; or that it might be traced to selfish influence which she was conscious of having often to resist in the advice of others, hurt her, even in her humility, and she writes:

"I make a distinction of late wherein I claim sympathy or counsel of earthly love or wisdom. In God-sent trials, or present troubles, I am as ready to claim it as any one, where I think my friend is ready to give it without adding too heavily to her own heavy cares or trials. I do not give voice to the mood of the moment often; to its weariness, its pain, its dread, even when I know hours of agony are before me, because I may be speaking or writing to some one who will share it too keenly with less strength perhaps than myself, or again when I know all the time that it is a transient evil, and by the time my cloud oppresses them it will have passed from me. Then there are some subjects which I can take to God alone; domestic grievances, should any such arise, injustice, things which human sympathy could not reach, or *when it would wrong another to claim it.* This I have learned by bitter experience, by having to strive for years, too often vainly, to rekindle the dead love of one person for another, destroyed at the first by my eager demand for justice, simple justice only to myself. I could forgive, I did do that, but —— never forgives. I kindled a fire I could not put out. Do you see? *I might have borne all these things in silence.* No, you cannot see. You have never had this terrible experience; but it has been one of the pangs of my life, and since then I have been shown *a more excellent way.*' I have found all the rest and sympathy, and justification of *self* that I could have needed, on my knees, often with bitter floods of tears, between me and God alone. He has taught me that it is no figure of speech, '*Come unto me, all ye that labor and are heavy laden.*'

"Do not think that I set myself up to do without human love and interest, or that I in the least undervalue it. You know that I have much more than most wives from my husband. You know, too, or if you don't I wish you did, how precious and helpful yours, and my mother's, and that of many others has been to me in my dark days; how at times I hunger and thirst after yours particularly, how gratefully it always comes to me. I almost despair of making you understand what I do mean. But *you know* how ready I am to give it. *Could one of my mother's children be otherwise! Do* I not strive '*to fulfil the law of Christ* in *the burden bearing of others*,' not only for those I love, but for every person, where I have even little or no personal interest. You have seen my life and its effort. You can tell."

There were circumstances which made it desirable that the coming winter should be passed in the country, but "The Willows" with its distance from the city and its proximity to the sea would be a trial to the health of both Mr. and Mrs. Haven, and they concluded to spend the winter in the city. They therefore came in town for the winter months with their children, fixing their residence in Sixteenth Street, in the neighborhood of St. George's Church. During the winter Mrs. Haven attended service there, whenever it was possible for her to go out. The force and fervor of Dr. Tyng's sermons, and the vigorous and wholesome activity of his life, inspired her with respect and affection. Her own practice for years had been an illustration of what he taught, and his earnest appeals to his congregation to the leading of a life energized by Christian love, stirred her as the sound of a trumpet quickens the blood in the veins of the spent soldier. In her letters to her friends she repeated these appeals, praying for blessings and long life for this preacher of righteousness.

On the 1st of December, 1862, she makes the following peculiar record. There are many of a similar character, showing how her faith and trust were continually rewarded till she had indeed "come to believe that she had all that she prayed for":

"While it is still fresh in my mind, let me put on record one of the sweetest tokens of God's goodness that I have ever received.

"When I began to work a little in the past summer, I hesitated as to whether I should work wholly on 'The Good Report,' which I was anxious to copy entirely myself, or write as I had at first intended, some magazine stories; for it was strange to me, and not quite comfortable, always to have no money of my own to fall back upon. I could do so little every day, only one hour's work, that I could accomplish but one of these things, and to help my decision came back the promise, '*Trust in the Lord and do good, and verily thou shalt be fed.*'

"So I trusted to Him, and, save the hospital story called 'One Day,' and a story for the Weekly, on the same subject, both of which grew naturally out of my hospital work—I wrote only on 'The Good Report.' But I was so well paid for my story, and S. has been so much prospered, that I have had abundantly all the money I could wish for myself and others.

"When I returned from Philadelphia last month, and fairly settled down for the winter, the same question came up for my Christmas money, for which I have always done some special writing, for I have been in the habit of making the most expensive purchases myself, besides what we did together. Our expenditure has been very great this year; extraordinary demands have been made upon our purses, and besides this I had my own special objects which S. might not think necessary.

"But then, if I wrote my stories, it would be after New Year's before I could get at my book, and I might be sick again, or die with it unaccomplished. As an answer again came, '*Trust in the Lord and be doing good trust also in Him and He shall bring it to pass.*' I hoped and believed that in writing this book, I *was doing good;* whether it ever came to any thing or not my motive was pure. So I trusted. I took up my book on the 13th day with great and renewed interest. I worked ten days. On Friday, the evening of the 21st, so soon!—S. said to me:

"'See, I have appropriated this to *your* Christmas expenses,' and he counted out nearly forty dollars into my hand.

"I received it with a mingling of pleasure and disappointment—pleasure because the means had been provided, disappointment because it would accomplish so small a part of what I intended. So I took it and thanked him, and said to myself, 'Well, if God does not send me any more, it is not right that I should do these things, though it seemed so.'

"S. watched my face for a few moments: 'You are disappointed. You are not obliged to me?'

"'Yes, dear, I am very much. I had no right to expect any thing.'

"'Why are you disappointed, then?'

"'Because it will not do all I wanted to do.'

"'What did you want to do?'

"'Oh, it does not matter since I cannot do it.'

"'But I want to hear,' and he took out a pencil and made me tell him the principal items. They came to over sixty dollars.

"'Well, I will not tease you any longer,' and he put another bill into my hands. 'I meant this for you too.'

"It was a bill for one hundred dollars. I gave one glance, and began to cry as usual. The revulsion overcame me, the seal of my rewarded trust was so wonderful.

"'What brings the tears?'

"It was a long time before I could tell him all, how, in the first place, I had trusted for the money, and left it all to Him. The signal answer to my faith, was as wonderful as if He had spoken directly to me from Heaven. Then there was the pleasure before me of accomplishing my wishes, but that was the very least. *He owned my work* as it were. He had sent me my wages, and if He accepted my book, He would bless it and make it useful as I have so long hoped and prayed.

"But it was also a pledge for the future. If He was faithful in that which was least, He would provide for my needs in greater things."

She goes on with a review of certain things which tried her faith very sorely, and had been making her heart very heavy, and she says:

"This was all natural, and very human, but here was a pledge to drive away my latest, most unspoken fears, and how could I but accept it, and be tearfully thankful, when my heart had for so many days carried and strug-g.ed with such a burden?

"So I put it on record as a help in some dark, distrustful day in the future, but chiefly to remember God's great and unmerited goodness, 'giving more than we can ask or think.'"

And she quotes, after this triumph of her faith, the beautiful metrical version of the 145th Psalm, "which brings back to me," she says, "so many happy Sunday afternoons in the dear little church at Mamaroneck."

# CHAPTER VIII.

## *HER LAST JOURNAL.*

"*Feb.* 16*th*, 1863.

"IT is a year ago to-day by the day of the month, since I lay so helpless and suffering at Mrs. F.'s. A year by the day of the week, since that Sunday noon, on which Dr. Parker told me that my life was in danger from seated disease of the lungs. I promised myself and my God if He would spare me a little longer to recover strength, that I would use every moment of the added time as a precious gift, and in His service. Especially to be more faithful in instructing and in praying for my children, and in helping others out of darkness into His light.

"In looking back on the year, in which not only has my life been spared so wonderfully, but my health in a great measure restored, and abundant, and heretofore unknown leisure secured to me, by the advice of my physicians, the record is one of unfaithfulness and shortcoming;

and of yielding too often to covert temptations to self-indulgence to which my position has peculiarly exposed me. I could not but be thankful for the abounding, and unlooked for blessings of the year, particularly for the health and strength of the present; and I desire in God's help to renew the vow of incessant faithfulness, especially in the care of my time, my health, and my duty to my children. I pray for a rich blessing '*of the best things* upon the friends whose roof protected me, whose thoughtful and unwearied attentions did so much for my restoration when I had so slight a claim on them. 'The blessing of the right and the left be upon them.'

"I arose this morning burdened with the many cares and anxieties coming from the proposed changes in our life, Sunday as it was! The inevitable cares and perhaps straightness of income, growing out of retirement from active business, vex and disturb me. Yet from the first we have tried to seek God's guidance, to say, '*if Thy presence go not with us carry us not up hence*,' and I know these distracting thoughts are mere human impatience, and the temptations to evil, to hinder me in present duty. It has been peculiarly so this morning, but I try to banish them by prayer, by recollections of the past, and its very manifest Divine guidances, some of them so wonderfully clear and plain.

"'Brought safely by His hand so far,
Why wilt thou now give place to fear?
How canst thou want if He provide,
Or lose thy way with such a guide?'

"Perhaps, too, the decision is not my affair after all. I have been so accustomed to take responsibility, that I may be thrusting myself forward in the place of S. now. I am called away, clearly called away, to other and absorbing interests. It may be all decided for me when I return. There is great comfort in believing that S. really does 'seek counsel' as well as myself, and this transaction may be wholly between his own soul and God.

"I have been greatly 'helped and strengthened,' as Mr. Gurney himself would have said, by my morning reading in the 'Life of J. J. Gurney.' The longer I live, the more I am persuaded that the Lord's children, unworthy as they are, are the objects not only of His spiritual grace, but of His especial Providence; that they are of more value in His sight than 'many sparrows,' and that 'the very hairs of our heads are numbered.' If this belief is well founded, if it is proved both by Scripture and experience, what a repose we may feel in the various turns and changes of our mortal pilgrimage. Truly '*all things shall work together for good to those that love God.*'

"In his after experience he thus depended upon the Divine guidance. When he became impressed with the belief that it was his duty to enter parliament, to bear Christian testimony before the English nation, he sought for every outward assistance to his judgment; yet was left clearly, by the advice of friends, and the power of circumstances, to follow his own choice. He feared lest 't should be only a temptation to draw him away from duties already accepted. Yet, on the other hand, if it were God's call to a new field of wider usefulness, he wished to accept it.

"'Deep has been my conflict,' he writes, 'in the fear of the enemy's snares. *I desire to be preserved in patience and simple dependence*, resting assured that the Lord will not leave me without a light to follow; that He will make an opening in His Providence for whatever is truly His own will concerning me. Or that, on the other hand, he will condescend to close every door through which the spirit forbids an entrance.'

"'I have had many anxious thoughts as to my future lot, and proceedings, and even conflicts between opposite views of duty; but I wholly believe that the Lord is graciously disposed to deal gently with me and permit me time to try the flame wet or dry, to go before me, and be my rearward.

"'We are on the wing this morning for Bayswater, trusting that a time of quietness of mind, and it may be some enjoyment in the Lord's service, awaits me. In the meanwhile, I leave events to work in that way which a good Providence may see fit to direct, being clear that my own course must at present be purely passive, and humbly trusting that my Divine and Holy Master will not leave His unworthy servant without help and guidance.'"

"I was never," says Mrs. Haven, "more fully persuaded of being sent on a message than in this visit to Boston. I go with a cheerful and tranquil mind now, leaving all in God's hands."

This visit to Boston was a matter of great moment to many persons. Her sister was there then, and with her two young persons, in whose care and welfare they were mutually interested. There was much to be talked about and decided upon, and the week spent there seemed all too short for its engagements. She also saw some old acquaintances, and made a few new ones. To all she bore the same impression. Her quick interest in every one, her sound judgment, her keen enjoyment, her words of counsel and comfort, added a new zest to every life with which hers came into contact. Going to a suburban town to dine with a connection, the drive on a wet day gave her some cold. She was a little hoarse on her return, and complained of her throat in the evening, but seemed very bright and almost gay, and would not admit that she was ill.

Speaking of singing—her favorite song was asked for, the last evening she was in Boston. She replied that she had no voice whatever, but "if they could endure the dismal croak which any attempt on her part at singing must be, she would try it." She went to the piano and sung the song of R. H. Stoddard's, which has been referred to, entitled

"THE TWO BRIDES.

"I saw two maids at kirk
And both were fair and sweet,
One in her wedding robe,
And one in her winding sheet.

"The chorister sung the hymn,
The sacred rites were read,
And one to Life for Life,
And one to Death, was wed.

"They were borne to their bridal beds,
In loveliness and bloom,
One in a merry castle,
The other a solemn tomb.

"One on the morrow awoke
To a world of sin and pain,
But the other was happier far,
And never woke again."

Alas! the music was gone from that voice forever on earth. The hoarseness never left her, and sometimes for days and weeks after this she could only speak in a whisper. Her letters, on her return to New York, were often prefaced in this way:

"I am forlorn to-day, with a new cold and quite hoarse, which I regret on ——'s account." "My throat prevents my going to see Mrs. C. about Mrs. E., as I hoped to." "Dr. S. says it is all climate; that I ought not to be here in March." "You will find lots of preaching in this envelope; but several things have done me so much good, that I could not help sharing the comfort with you." "I said to S. a night or two ago:

"'How often we are kept up and quieted by plans that seem the best things, but which are not the ones Providence is preparing for us or designs us to have. How one plan which never was adopted, stood between me and despair for a month or two.' When I heard that your wishes in regard to sending B. away were frustrated, I felt at once that it was because some better purpose still for him existed in God's providence, to be known in good time; to be asked for in faith perhaps, and to be depended upon, since all our earthly wisdom seemed to be wrapped up in that one plan. My throat is hateful again. I don't know but I must stay in the house till we are done with snow."

In regard to their arrangements for the future, which had disturbed her so, she writes in her journal:

"*March 22d.*

"For the present, at least, we are to return to 'The Willows.' I found it decided for me on my return from Boston, so I had nothing to do but 'to sit still.'"

After enumerating the advantages of keeping "The Willows" for their summer residence, she says:

"The change in the winter brings change of scene, prevents morbid forecasting, and gives opportunity for daily exercise in the open air. When I incline to be restless and impatient about the final issue, I see the message still, '*in quietness and confidence shall be your strength.*'"

During Lent of this year her mind and heart were full of concern for the beloved little church in Mamaroneck where she had so long worshipped, for its pastor, for whom her respect and affection were very sincere, as the whole of her life as a parishioner, and as many references in her letters and journal testify, and for the people with and for whom she had so long prayed. She prays now that "after a long drouth, the spirit of God may be plentifully poured out upon them."

"I have found two helpful things in my morning reading, both marked long ago.

"'*They helped every one, his neighbor and every one said to his brother, be of good courage.*'

"'*So the carpenter encouraged the goldsmith, and he that smote with the hammer, him that smote with the anvil, saying,*' etc.

"'*Fear not for I am with thee; fear not, be not dismayed, for I am thy God. I will strengthen thee, yea, I will help thee, yea, I will uphold thee.*'

"'*When the poor and needy seek water, and there is none, and their tongue faileth for thirst, I, the Lord, will hear them; I the God of Israel will not forsake them.*'

"'*I will open rivers in high places, and fountains in the midst of the valley; I will make the wilderness a pool of water, and the dry land springs of water.*'

"I was obliged to leave church this morning from faintness, to my great disappointment, but I was repaid, in the little time that I was there, for the effort of going, by this additional helpful, and very familiar text in the morning lesson: Haggai ii. 4. Perhaps the first part of the chapter gives the reason for this long drouth, and my repeated disappointments. Selfish prayers for husband, wife, child, or friend, are refused and rebuked by failure and disappointment, because we have not the interest of God's church, His house, at heart until we have less 'narrow prayers,' take up His cause heartily, and receive all at once."

She records at some length another instance of remarkable answer to prayer in her own experience, and then says:

"Answered again 'in that which is least,' let me see in it a pledge 'of that which is greatest.'

"I have had a nice morning, though quite ill, finding

so much encouragement for the country's peace and the whole world's conversion from rebellion against God's laws. How wonderful that this should come also!"

"*April 4d*, EASTER EVE.

"Lent going out in a heavy storm of rain, sleet, and snow. I proposed to myself at its commencement several distinct subjects for prayer. I have kept as usual an unfaithful watch. Yet God may even now grant me my heart's desire, undeserved as it is. It is never of our deserving, but of His mercy. Therefore I hope that F—— may be led into the way of true peace; that S. may grow in grace and in the knowledge of our Lord Jesus Christ; that N—— may be strengthened and confirmed, and brought nearer to the Heavenly Father, by His loving kindness; that B—— may receive the baptism of a deep repentence and a true conversion; that our land may be restored to peace and prosperity, and we be made, by our trials, a God-fearing and honoring nation; that His kingdom may come in all the world; also I pray anxiously for my beloved church and pastor.

"I have had the fifty-fifth chapter of Isaiah for my evening lesson, full of promises for all these things, espe cially the last two verses.

"I leave all in God's hands, all for His own good time and way. I find this is not my first watch for F——. God has granted me all else—why not this?

"The sleety storm goes on. Before the verses I have quoted is this, most appropriate for the day: 'For as the rain cometh down, and the snow from Heaven, and returneth not thither, but watereth the earth and maketh it bring forth and bud, that it may give seed to the sower and bread to the eater.'

"'*So shall my word be that goeth forth out of my mouth. It shall not return unto me void, but it shall accomplish that which I please, and it shall prosper in the thing whereto I sent it.*'

"God's word is the means of accomplishing the change we desire in the hearts and lives of men; but as the snow and the rain sink into the ground, and become forgotten influences, though not the less vital and sure; bringing the thing to pass in proper, or ordered time and season; so with this fertilizing, nourishing, transforming power.

"*We* give the credit to the sunshine of providential circumstances, which brings the bud to blossom, the fruit to maturity."

Except her letters, she wrote nothing more. How full her heart was for others! How broad and all-embracing her Christian love and charity, this last record shows. What was left of life and strength was given as freely as her prayers.

In spite of the remonstrances of her friends she had charged herself with the preparation of the spring wardrobes of two young relations, in addition to all that her own family required.

She was unable to walk, but she drove out day after day to attend to these things; sometimes spending a whole morning in the carriage, and interesting herself in all the minutiæ of the work. Her extraordinary energy constantly sought fresh objects on which to expend itself, and never seemed to fail till she was laid upon her couch.

She consulted with writers and publishers about new editions of favorite books, wrote many letters connected with such business, recommended plans which seemed to her to promise success, hurried some who would possibly be late in getting a book ready for the press in time for the fall issue; and thus interested and occupied herself when able to be off her couch, till the time came for them to return to "The Willows."

To those who watched her during the latter years of her life, when heart and brain were always busy with the interests of others, who saw her use her pen till it fell from fingers too weak to hold it longer, who heard her plead the cause of others while she had a voice to speak, who saw lips move in inarticulate prayer when the low voice had almost left her, who counted every effort by which she thus exhausted her ebbing life with the breathless anxiety of agonized love—to all such there is a thought of consolation in lines recently written of her by one who was reading tearfully her last published volume:

"I know she sees how many hearts
  Have thrilled to purer thought,
Touched by the holy sympathies
  Her blessed life has taught.

"I know that every gentle word
  Traced amid care and pain,
Wrought into jewels, shines upon
  Her angel robes again;
That in the New Jerusalem
  No whiter soul is there,
Than hers who fashioned life with faith,
  And ended it with prayer."

# CHAPTER IX.

## *LAST LETTERS.*

THE letters to her friends at this time, all expressing the most lively interest in their affairs, which were instinctively confided to her, seem wonders of wisdom in the counsel she gave, and almost inspired benedictions. To one who was in great trouble, she writes:

"Some time ago we took for our year's motto, '*Be careful of nothing, but in every thing by prayer and supplication, with thanksgiving, let your requests be made known unto God.*' I, at least, realized the promise following, '*and the peace of God which passeth all understanding shall keep your hearts and minds through Christ Jesus.*'

"It has been a time, however, of comparative personal rest. I often wonder how I shall bend to the stream of trouble when it rises again, loss of home, or children, or husband, or means to do for others, or especially the sufferings of those I love. I should despair of being brave but for the promise, '*God is faithful.*' Perhaps I shall be unfaithful, and take myself out of His hands; that is all I dread.

"May you, dear N——, 'increasing in the knowledge of God, be strengthened with all might according to His glorious power, unto all patience, and long suffering, with joyfulness.' What more can I say? I often think of the disciples at the Transfiguration, 'and *they feared as they entered into the cloud.*' But '*there came a voice out of the cloud saying: This is my beloved Son, hear Him.*' I have always found that I learn more of the Beloved Son when the cloud overshadows me, much as I dread to enter it, and that I listen more willingly to His voice. I have some verses half planned, with that thought. Do you like it? Does it give you comfort? I may have seen it somewhere before.

"This letter, so far, might be called 'Scripture readings,' but I don't know how else to attempt to meet the throng of adversities that seem to hem you in; and you will understand, I know."

Just before they left for the country she wrote to a dear friend in the city who was also an invalid:

"I did not think, my dear C——, that so many days would have passed before I acknowledged your little basket of 'immortelles,' a surprise and a pleasure to receive. I believe it is the only material keepsake I have from you save your picture. But I shall never *need* a remembrance, glad as I am to have this. You were continually in my mind during Lent, and more particularly in Passion week. I started on Good Friday afternoon to go over to see you, but the wind was uncommonly cold, and my throat very raw; besides, I had elected all along to go over on Easter Even, *in memoriam* of the walk we took to St. Peter's together, in the evening, so many years ago; so I turned back, and the next day was stormy, and then weakness, and illness, and so on—and on—till now.

"How much I thought of you then, always suffering, always having suffered '*in the flesh*,' aye, and in spirit too! May God give you patience as He has done, and trust in the wisdom and love that cannot err, though doubt and weariness rise up to deny it!

"I had two or three dreadful nights, and in one I remember with what a flash of comfort came the thought, '*Who spared not His own Son;*' and what must sin be, or rather what must it not be, when such an expiation is required!

"May God be with you day and night on your bed of suffering. May Christ and the Comforter abide with you always; may angel's care minister to you until you shall come *where the inhabitants shall no more say*, '*I am sick, neither shall there be any more pain.*'

"Will you thank your husband for the Report, which I have read with much interest, and for his note, and his trouble regarding the tract. Tell him to take no further trouble. If he thinks it might be useful, I will have another edition printed at my own expense, and send it to the Commission; but I feel so uncertain of its value. I suppose I ought to act on faith, and the remembrance *of the cup of cold water.*"

In May they left their city home, but their own home, which had been for some time undergoing repairs, was not yet ready for them, and they stayed a short time at a house in the neighborhood, where Mr. H. could superintend the last preparations for the reëntrance to "The Willows." From this place she writes:

"I dare say you will think I am lost, but I have been used up for several days, suffering from such repeated and prolonged attacks of faintness that I dared not go out. Some days these continue all day, in others they pass off in the morning; they are accompanied by spasms, from indigestion I suppose."

And then follow *several pages* of business matters, chiefly planning for the comfort of others. Again:

"With S., who cannot bear to see me exerting myself, out of the way, and my morning agony over, I will try to say two words or so. I tried to write all last week, but was very sick with rush of blood from the heart to the head, alternating with faintness, partly produced by 'starvation.' Meat and bread are all that agree with me, and these I cannot eat; my throat is in such a state that soft boiled eggs and cream are all I can swallow, and these I cannot digest.

"To-day I must really say, 'Thank God I am much more comfortable.' My voice is quite audible, which is encouraging, as it is damp, and an easterly wind.

"I had no idea I had so little patience and endurance for bodily pain. I thought I could be very heroic, but I believe more than ever that we never know ourselves. This illness has taught me several lessons; but oh! I forget so fast! I thought last year if I could only be spared for the children I would be so faithful, but I was not. I do not suppose I shall be now, but I *mean* to be, 'sick bed' resolution as it is. All this *about myself*, my favorite topic of late."

Again:

"I don't know whether I ought to write to you today after all. This long storm has depressed me, and the lack of fresh air and exercise has added to my discomfort, that when I have said that the dampness has made my throat worse, I have said the worst of myself. I was getting on nicely when this storm set in, with the change of air, scene, and food, and hope to do so again in the sunshine. I suppose mother has told you what a serious attack I have had; I felt so very ill as I finished my last letter to you, that but for croaking, I should have said that *I believed I was going out with the tide.* I know I meant it as I wrote that last sentence, and in all the bodily suffering I ever endured, nothing ever went beyond it. My heart seemed to have been paralyzed, but its action is somewhat restored.

"I am just as far as possible from your sisterly idea of 'doing my best for everybody.' I do nothing for anybody. I do not even care for myself, but lie hours together on the bed or sofa, in the most utter do-nothingness that I ever arrived at. I can scarcely believe it, or understand how so short an illness could so use up my strength."

They had now reëntered "The Willows," which had been enlarged and repaired. The grounds were in most perfect order, and the winter in town had prepared Mrs. Haven for the keenest enjoyment of home comforts. As a surprise for her, her husband had very elegantly, and with especial regard to her peculiar tastes, refurnished her own room. She said characteristically:

"The night before we went into our own home I was very sleepless, so I lay awake, planning the changes in the ordering of the furniture necessary from increased room. The first night I spent there I lay awake thinking sadly how much the money spent in that luxurious furnishing would have done for so many who were needing help."

She could not be insensible or ungrateful to the love which had surrounded her now, by the grace and beauty which she had so long denied to the tastes which always craved such things. She writes:

"All my life long I have loved beautiful and dainty things, and have never had the opportunity to indulge my taste; indeed I had entirely given up the thought, or longing I might call it, till this summer every one conspires to indulge me. The house outside and in, my lovely room, the out-of-door beauty everywhere. I cannot tell you what delight and enjoyment I take in them all."

As the weather became suitable she ventured out a few times about the grounds, her sweet face protected by a dainty hood, and a fleecy Shetland shawl wrapped about her wasted figure.

Once she took courage and went into town, partly to see her physician and partly to carry out one of her favorite projects; for despite her protest she was still planning the comfort and welfare of others. She had been very anxious for a friend to have a sewing machine, and had arranged that it should be a gift to her. She made an appointment to meet her at the establishment of Wheeler & Wilson, that she might witness the pleasure and surprise the gift would bring, as she received one of their most beautifully-finished and elegantly-cased instruments. A ruling passion indeed, strong to the last, was this of serving others! But the ride to town, and the excitement attending her visit, were too much for her strength. In the suffering that followed she confessed to this.

It was here, and of this last visit, that a gentleman said on her leaving the place, "The sun seems to go under a cloud as she goes out." With the kind smile on her lip, and the light in her eye kindled by her genial interest in every thing, in every person, even in the transaction of business, she did indeed bring sunshine with her. She awoke a true feeling of friendship in hearts that too often closed in their counting-rooms to every thing but business and its selfish engrossments.

"Toward the latter part of her life," said a gentleman with whom she had only business relations, "she seemed to me as I talked with her

16*

to have a halo about her, as the old saints are painted."

Then her sympathies with others, and her interest in them, was so infectious. She appeared to take it for granted that all felt as kindly, and were as glad of the opportunity to do good as she was; and very shame not infrequently broke through the crust of selfishness, and dissipated churlishness, bringing out a man's heart and better feeling as she appealed in behalf of any cherished interest she was trying to promote. She had the tact in which many who are generous themselves are quite deficient. She could appeal so effectually, that she really taught the pleasure of service rendered, to some, the centre and circumference of whose life was *self.*

The "good in every thing" was ever apparent to her spiritual vision. One of her latest letters to her sister was in this wise:

"You and W. will find the use of these years of discipline through the perverseness and ungenerousness of others, and the combination of cares and trials. 'Fit for the Master's use,' and now He appoints the service. It is strange as my days of active service end, that yours commence. Your true sphere will be found and widen before you as mine closes. *I am content.* I could not once have said this, to be laid aside and see others allowed to do what my hands no longer may."

In despite of pain and weariness, of days of intense suffering which no human love was powerful to soothe, these last weeks held much joy and peace in them. Her heart was always full of thankfulness for the slightest alleviation to her pain. Her enjoyment often far outbalanced her suffering; her very last letter to her sister began, "This is a heavenly day in a heavenly place."

## CHAPTER X.

### *LAST HOURS.*

THESE cannot be better depicted than by her beloved "Marie E.," whose privilege it was to be beside her in those sacred moments, and to minister to her last earthly needs.

"On the 21st of July her baby-girl was born; and after that it was hoped that her disease would be arrested, and health restored. But the fair little child throve and grew strong while the mother drooped and failed. There was a brief rallying, the last flashing upward of the wasting flame when the baby was a few weeks old. But the false hope was too quickly dashed, and a few weeks more found the little new-comer motherless, the household desolate, and life robbed of what seemed its sole treasure to one who

> 'Will miss her, and go mourning
> All his solitary days.'

"On Wednesday, August 19th, she had been lifted from the bed to a large easy-chair in which she was accustomed to sit for a little while every day. Resting among the soft pillows, wrapped in a Shetland shawl, and her exquisite hands folded across her prayer-book, open at *the Litany*, she never looked lovelier, it seemed to those who lingered beside her. Her eyes were full of tender light, her cheeks flushed with the hectic that brings such fatal beauty, and the rich masses of her hair shading her wasted temples, all combined to make up a picture of such exceeding loveliness as will never fade from the memories of those who gazed upon it.

"Its sweet repose lasted but for a very brief space. A fit of coughing, or rather an attempt to cough, resulted in a suffocating spasm of the throat; and for a time which none measured, its duration seemed ages rather than moments, the very pangs of death were suffered in their sharpest form. Wasted and weakened by her long suffering, the physical agony seemed almost to overpower even her faith; and the despairing cry, 'I am dying! oh, pray that it may be short. Oh, my God, let it be short,' was too full of anguish to be remembered calmly.

"Thank God the prayers were heard; relief was granted, and for a little while she was given back to the love that clung to her so desperately. Through the night following she lay awake much of the time murmuring repeatedly words of prayer and grateful acknowledgment for the deliverance that had been sent her.

"'It was all needed,' she said once, 'every pang. But I was so weak, I thought I could not bear it. God was better than I deserved; He has spared my life.'

"At another time she asked, in a half wandering way, waking from a brief sleep:

"'Do you believe there is really a God who is our Father? who loves us, and cares about us always?'

"'I do not believe, *I know*,' was the reply. 'And so do you, Alice. No one knows it so well as you.'

"'Oh yes, surely!' she exclaimed with a lovely smile, consciousness and memory flashing back. 'The *everlasting arms*, they are bearing me upward now.'

"Bending over her at another time in the darkness, one who watched her heard her whisper:

"'I thank Thee, oh my Heavenly Father, for all Thy dear love. I thank Thee for my precious husband and dear children. *I thank Thee for all my agonizing suffering.*'

"Three days more were all that remained of life, or suffering to her, and of the latter it pleased God to spare her much. She slept or was unconscious a great deal of the time, mind and body growing weaker together as her feet drew nearer the brink of the Dark River. On Saturday, toward nightfall, the Death Angel made his presence felt in the shadowy room. But he came gently, not with pain or terror. The anguish of that extreme hour was all for those who watched the failing breath and fading eyes, not for her in whom the awful change was taking place in such serene silence. No further agony of the wasted form and weary spirit was allowed; and hour after hour stole softly by while the calm sweetness of her rest was undisturbed by any passing pain. The murmured words that dropped from lips half unconscious, told only of love and happiness; and while the solemn shadow of that unseen Mystery brooded above, the heavenly light of 'the peace that passeth all understanding,' made her face 'as it were the face of an angel.'

"None of those who stood by that death-bed will ever forget its holy serenity, least of all the ineffable beauty of that supreme moment which marked

'The passing of the sweetest soul
That ever looked with human eyes.'

"No words could picture the sudden rapture that illuminated the whole countenance, flashed out from eyes we had thought closed in slumber, gleamed across lips that seemed sealed from smiling for ever more. It was as though the realization of what 'eye hath not seen, nor ear heard, nor hath it entered into the heart of man to conceive' was revealed in one unutterable vision. The tear-blinded eyes fixed upon hers might not behold what she beheld, but they saw its glory reflected for one brief moment, never to be forgotten till the veil of this mortality is withdrawn, and we also behold 'The King in His beauty.'"

How better can we picture the desolation that followed than in these lines, written years before by her who had 'calmly gone unto her rest,' with stricken hearts throbbing about her; a prophetic picture of her own home on this lovely Sunday morning, August 23d, 1863:

"Shut out the sunlight from the room,
I cannot bear its splendor,
While tears for one so young so true,
A mournful tribute render.

"I'm thinking of that silent hour
When last she smiled a blessing
To the young children at her side,
Who came with sweet caressing.

"When eyes of love beheld in her
The sum of earthly treasure,
And a manly heart thanked God who gave
Such gladness in such measure.

"Ah me, how dark that pleasant room
Where now her form is lying!
The laughter has to wailing changed,
The smiles give place to sighing.

"The little ones with linked hands,
And voices low with weeping,
Come softly to the narrow couch
To see their mother sleeping.

'They wonder at the rigid form,
Death's icy touch revealing,
And ask why still the heavy lids
Her soft eyes are concealing.

"No pressure answers from the lips
  That, in their childish error,
They fondly kiss, then shrink away
  With new and nameless terror.

"Her hands are folded on her breast,
  Yet in their silent clasping,
There seems a prayer for those she leaves,
  Comfort and guidance asking.

"Accept the token while ye weep,
  And stricken hearts are throbbing;
She goeth calmly unto rest,
  The grave of terror robbing.

"To her the dusky gate of death
  Is now no fearful portal,
Earth's keenest pangs are all forgot
  In joys of life immortal."

The same hand that gave us the record of the death-bed scene, has described that which was witnessed in the church where she had long worshipped "in the beauty of holiness."

"One word more we must claim for a passing glimpse at the funeral services, rendered with rare beauty and harmony. In the simple village church, before the altar where she had knelt so many years, they placed the casket that held all that remained of a jewel too precious for our keeping. Rare flowers, only less exquisite than the face they encircled, the hands in which they were clasped, were heaped about her in lavish loveliness;

for friends and neighbors had vied with each other to adorn her death, even as they had done to gladden her life, with these sweet tokens of their reverent love. One fair hand held sprigs of heliotrope and violets placed there by the little fingers of her children, their usual morning tribute, and now their last; but the other clasped, lying upon her breast a cross of snow white, fragrant flowers. All her life long she had clung 'simply to Thy cross;" it was fitting that she should hold the pale emblem in death, as all felt when that sweetest of hymns 'Rock of ages, cleft for me,' swelled in its soft minors through the church.

"Seldom at any funeral have been gathered so many brought together by one sincere impulse of love and sympathy. In the throng of earnest faces not one careless, or indifferent gazer, could be seen; young and old, rich and poor, met together in common sorrow, for all in the parish counted her as a friend. And the tears that rained from so many eyes, and the sobs that shook even manly breasts, as they drew near for one last look at that placid face, bore witness to the universal love and reverence she had inspired. But one emotion prevailed in all that multitude; they wept together as a bereaved household mourning its dearest ornament and joy.

"The pastor who had baptized her children, one after another, and 'broken the bread of life' to her kneeling by these chancel rails where now her coffin stood, read the solemn and beautiful burial service above her head. And the friend of her childhood, the brother-in-law whose love had followed her in every event of her whole life, and who had thus a still nearer and dearer right to share in this sacred office, spoke the fitting and expressive eulogy which will be remembered long by all who were present, for its eloquence and indescribable tenderness, as well as its deep truthfulness to her character.

"We are fain to linger over this closing scene, beautiful beyond any idea that our poor words have given; inasmuch as it was in perfect harmony with a life whose beauty has rarely been equalled."

When they left the church all that was mortal of Alice Haven was borne to the quiet little burial ground of Rye, where her last resting-place is marked by a cross, as was her own wish, bearing simply her name and age, and the words so often uttered by her lips, and which she illustrated through all her life:

"BEAR YE ONE ANOTHER'S BURDENS, AND SO FULFIL THE LAW OF CHRIST."

# CONCLUSION.

A THRILL of sorrow and sympathy went through the country when on the morning of the 24th of August, the readers of the New York "World" learned of the death of "Cousin Alice" in the following obituary notice:

"In the simple announcement in our obituary column this morning, of the death of *Alice B. Haven*, many of our readers will find an interest, the deeper and sadder for their knowledge that it chronicles the departure from earth of one of its most gifted and lovely daughters known to a multitude of our readers as 'Cousin Alice.'

"Mrs. Haven was yet in the prime of life, not having completed her thirty-sixth year. For more than half of her days she has been achieving her reputation as a pure and charming writer for the young, and has won for herself a place among the poets of the land by not a few lofty and enduring lyrics.

"Admirable and highly cherished as her fame in the world of letters will be, this is, however, the least excellence of her now sacred memory. The crown of her character was her truly unselfish and unsparing consecration to the highest good of others, not only of those who had natural claims upon her but of all who came within the reach of her hand and her influence.

"She spent and was spent for the promotion of pure religion and sweet practical virtue. In her the church found a faithful adherent and auxiliary, and charity a blessed exemplar and almoner. Her bereaved home and family will mourn her only more in degree, than the parish and the people, who will know her no more in her unostentatious and almost uncircumscribed ministries of love. Beyond these a wide circle of the public will miss her ever fresh and fragrant contributions to sacred and secular literature alike.

"Her beautiful life-service is ended apparently in the midst of its sweet and pure liturgy; but God and the angels have uttered its *Amen*."

In the same paper appeared from the same pen a fitting

"IN MEMORIAM.

"The silver cord is loosed whereon were strung
The priceless pearls of an unsullied life;
And while the jewels drop, our hearts are rife
With anguish from their grieving tendrils wrung—

That grew and twined about that slender string,
As if it held a cable's strength instead;
Half of our wealth is lost since she is dead—
Whose virtues to contempt our best deeds bring.
No more, alas! that cord of pearls shall hang
For rare adornment, Earth's fair neck around;
Its silver brightness hid beneath the ground;
And every scattered pearl for us a pang,
Yet Memory's hand shall gather them again
And bind them on our hearts, a holy endless chain.

"W. C. R."

Mrs. Haven was buried in the secluded Cemetery of Rye in accordance with her own wish. She had a strong preference for a quiet country burial place, and some years before had expressed the feeling in a poem which she had written with reference to the New York Bay Cemetery, entitled,

"BEAR OUT THE DEAD."

Aye! carry out your dead!
They have won *rest;*
Theirs was the burden, and the heat of day,
Now smooth the shining hair, the white hands lay
Folded upon the breast.

The fluttering heart is still!
No hope, no care!
In moveless calm, the labored throbbings cease;
The marble forehead bears the seal of peace,
Its smile, the lips still wear.

Therefore, " bear out the dead."
Far from the strife
That daily soundeth through the city streets,
Where momently the burdened air repeats
The hurried march of life.

"Nay," some true mourner saith,
"In hallowed ground
We make their graves, in shade of cross or spire,
Where chime and prayer, and chaunt of solemn choir
Thrill with a dirge-like sound."

Or others grieving pray—
"Not out of sight
Make the low mound, but where our feet may tread
Daily, in loving memory of the dead,
Who were life's chief delight."

Think you our anthems reach
Where that "*new song*"
As noise of many waters surging rolls?
Our earthly prayers though wrung from anguished souls
They hear where angels throng?

And when another love
Shall fill the heart
Now void and desolate, these graves will lie
O'ergrown, or trampled down by passers-by,
In crowded church or mart.

For traffic in due time
Will covet this—
The narrow space which grudgingly is given,
Pent under walls which bar the light of Heaven,
The sunshine's gentle kiss.

Therefore, "bear out the dead"
Where earthly calm
May image that which they have surely won,
Where careless feet the hallowed paths shall shun,
Nor idle hands work harm.

Daisies and violets,
The snow white rose,
With trailing ivy o'er the earth shall wreathe,
And solemn chants the lingering south winds breathe,
Where fir or cypress grows.

No taint of sin or shame
The rippling tide
Bears from the distant city clearly seen,
The waters roll their clear, bright waves between,
And life from death divide.

They ask this rest of thee
All faith to prove,
In the fair stillness eloquent to teach
The Sabbath calm of Heaven surpassing speech,
The dead ye mourn and love.

From every direction the most loving and reverential tributes were poured forth to the memory of one whom all claimed as a friend, and to whom many looked up as a benefactress. Letters were addressed to her husband and family, in some cases by those who were personally strangers to them; tributes were paid in newspapers and magazines, in prose and verse, and the characteristics of these were that even more love and appreciation of the devoted and high-minded Christian woman and self-sacrificing friend was evident in these innumerable tributes than apprehension of the comprehensive and fine intellect which had made her heart offerings so well known and widely spread.

It is impossible to give all these, but from them we select a few which will be read with interest: The first is from a letter addressed by her pastor, the Rev. John Ward, to her sister

"I am happy to add my testimony to the rare excellence and exalted worth of character possessed by Mrs. Haven. I feel it to have been a privilege to have had her for a parishioner, such as rarely falls to the lot of a country clergyman. In a parish and neighborhood so circumscribed as this, full scope could not be afforded for powers so great, and energies so untiring as hers. Yet in every thing in which the cause of the church, the advancement of true religion, and the good of society were concerned, *she* was ever foremost; and with that sweet persuasiveness of manners so especially her own, she overcame obstacles, and effected results, such as few could have accomplished.

"Confirmations in the parish were to her, seasons of peculiar interest, and her coöperation in preparing the candidate for assuming the obligations of Baptism with intelligence and serious devotion of heart, was most gratefully appreciated. In the Confirmation season to which you refer, and in which there seemed to prevail in the parish a more general feeling of the importance of religious duties, she was most untiring in her efforts to assist me; and in some cases which required to be approached with peculiar tact and gentleness, the fruits, I am persuaded, were the harvest of her prayers and efforts.

"She particularly impressed me with her conscientious observance of the Lord's day, so faithfully fulfilling the injunction, 'Remember the Sabbath day to keep it holy.' She did indeed 'stand up for God,' and was found in His Temple when her health would have been deemed by many a sufficient excuse for her remaining at home, and when her devoted and earnest manner impressed all that her's was no lip service, but the homage of a heart lifted in grateful praise, or bowed in lowliest breath of prayer; listening, too, to teachings, which if they seemed feeble to her, she yet received as from one whom she felt to be an ambassador from his Master and hers.

"Knowing Mrs. Haven's many social and literary engagements, I called less frequently than my inclinations prompted, but I always left her strengthened for my labor, and inspired by her zeal which had no limit, but the salvation of all with whom she came in contact.

"If I should attempt to speak of her charities, and her

efforts to ameliorate the condition of the poor in the village, I might fill pages.

"Drawing from the fountain of her Christian benevolence, she literally obeyed the Divine injunction, 'Never turn thy face away from any poor man,' and the kindly words of sympathy and counsel with which her charities were accompanied, have caused her to be remembered with a most reverential affection. 'Many shall rise up and call her blessed.'

"As an instance of the admiration and love with which she was regarded, a devoted member of the Romish Church said, at her funeral, 'If Mrs Haven has not gone to Heaven, no one need try to.'

"She was certainly that noblest type of woman, *the Christian woman.* One who wore always the badge of her profession, and like the Apostle, felt the cross to be her chiefest glory. *This* I think was the secret of the great influence which she exerted in the society in which she moved; the beautiful consistency of character that showed her to be the *Christian* at all times and in all places, and above all her beautiful example as a humble and devoted follower of the lowly Jesus, which made so many willing to be led by her whose hold they saw was so firm upon the Rock of Ages."

From the various notices which appeared in the leading magazines, we select one from the pen of Miss Virginia Townsend, one of the editors of Arthur's Home Magazine, which is particularly interesting, because it refers to an incident which illustrates an eminent characteristic of Mrs. Haven, her broad sympathy, and untiring effort to serve others:

"The closing days of the last summer carried to many a home and heart throughout the land a message of grief whose memory will not easily pass away.

"The life of Mrs. Alice B. Haven closed just before the summer's did. There seemed some peculiar fitness in their going out so closely together—the service of both completed; the voices of both falling into eternal silence; and both lingering in our memories like the tones of some sweet singer which we may never hear again, but which we shall carry in our thoughts through all our lives.

"It does not become the writer of this to furnish these pages with a biographical sketch of Mrs. Haven. Those who knew her intimately as wife and mother, and sister and friend, have elsewhere performed that work, and briefly told us how nobly she fulfilled all the public and private duties of her life, faithfully and humbly seeking to infuse into all the spirit of a true Christian womanhood.

"But a single incident which came to the writer's knowledge, and which touchingly illustrates the scope and tenor of the life of Mrs. Haven, will not only be welcomed by many readers who loved her work, and mourn her loss, but through it, though tender voice and faithful pen are hushed now, she may speak to some heart that shall be encouraged to 'go and do likewise.'

"It is more than six years ago since Mrs. Haven, during a brief visit to Philadelphia, heard her friend, Mr. Louis A. Godey, mention the name of a young lady who had occasionally contributed to his magazine, and who, herself on a visit to the city, found suddenly a new and wider sphere of literary usefulness opening before her.

"The quick sympathies of Mrs. Haven enlisted her interest at once in one, whose writings she had occasionally seen, and for whose future her generous nature felt a keen solicitude.

"An interview with the young lady was easily obtained, and *she* will never cease to remember the impression of Mrs. Haven's face and voice as she entered the parlor. There was so much cordial animation in her greeting, so much tender interest in those beautiful dark eyes, and oh! so much kindly and faithful counsel in the words that fell a little later from the lips which seemed pendulous betwixt smiles and sadness, that that hour or two will never be forgotten by the listener who hung on every tone and expression, and tried to catch the spirit and import of each; and if she did not succeed then, she did afterwards when a sterner teacher revealed them.

"An interview like this must from its very nature be a confidential one, reaching beyond externals, to somewhat that is essential and vital.

"It is sufficient to say, that Mrs. Haven fancied her young friend's position had at that moment some general likeness to certain phases of her own experience, and that her wider knowledge of the world and of some peculiar paths of temptation and danger would furnish those practical warnings and suggestions, of which a young sister-writer might greatly stand in need.

"But how few of her sex would have had the heart, the courage, or the tact to offer these as *she* did!

"Sometimes as she touched on her own life, the tears stood still in those large, steadfast, beautiful eyes; sometimes smiles, swift and bright as a child's, flashed out from a face that seemed still in the light of its early twenties, a face beautiful in itself, growing doubly so to the gazer through all its infinite charm and grace of expression.

"The interview closed at last, regretfully on one side at least. The paths of these two, singular to say, never intersected again, although both I believe separated with the hope and expectation of subsequent meetings which various small obstacles prevented.

"As the years grew, however, bringing with them the experience which makes us all sadder, and if lived in any true sense, wiser; the real purpose and significance of Mrs. Haven's visit manifested itself to her who received it. But a letter written to Mrs. Haven out of the gratitude of her heart, was after awhile replied to, with that complete and final answer which sooner or later, oh, my reader, must be the last story which can be told of you, or me, 'She is dead!'

"'Dead and yet speaking' by her life of love and sacrifice, of service and faithfulness, speaking in a thousand incidents such as this, that may never be written in any book save that one wherein are the chapters of every human life.

"How many women are there, who would have had the care, or taken the pains to turn aside from the pleasure and excitement of a brief social visit, to a stranger sister, whose feet were just about entering some untried path, wherein it was likely might lie much stress and trial for her? And of few of us may it be said as of her, 'Her life had no ignoble days.'

"That pen whose genius was dedicated to the service of God and the good of man, lies silent; it will gladden and exalt us no more with its sweet stories of human life, of trial, of sacrifice, of faith, and of the joy and beauty of endurance and endeavor, amid the strain of care and wearing details of life; no more sweet, and living home pictures, will brighten along her swift pen; the small white hand which held it so long, and so bravely, now lies silent and cold under the smooth linen of these winter snows. Like the light of the summer days amid which she faded, has the noble and loving woman with her rare gifts of mind and heart passed away.

"From the shadows of the little church at Mamaroneck, they bore all that was mortal of Alice B. Haven; but the seed which she scattered prayerfully along her earthly path shall take deep root by the water courses of other lives, and it shall not be gathered in the harvests that are of this world."

In "The Christian Times," published at

Chicago, appeared the following, one of many more or less extended obituaries which the newspapers for weeks after her death brought to the public, witnessing how her works praised her of whom they wrote.

"ALICE B. HAVEN.

BY MRS. MARY C. VAUGHN.

"As I prepare my pen and seat myself to write, there comes to me tidings of the death of one well known to the reading public, but not more admired for her talents than beloved by a large circle of deeply-attached friends. A beautiful life was hers; *a life that perhaps suppressed its largest capacities*, but put prominently forward only those that were pure and true. There is in our day a powerful temptation ever placed before writers. By pandering to a low taste, there is to be gained both money and popularity; by letting the imagination run riot in producing sensational articles, stories, sketches, or brochures of the Fanny Fern style, for example, there is to be obtained a certain notoriety which all cannot see is even more ephemeral than life itself—a blaze of the ascending rocket sure to be followed by the dull *thud* of the falling stick. By indulging in sarcasm, by striving to say the wittiest and bitterest things of every human being and institution, by forgetting the chiefest of virtues, *charity*, the writer may gain *fame*, of a certain sort.

"But Alice B. Haven turned from such temptations, firmly and courageously. Her talents were dedicated to a high purpose, not merely to amuse and interest, though she seldom failed to do that, but to warn, to instruct, to inculcate some important lesson, to paint some worthy moral. She did not invade the realm of the preacher; her field was rather the minor morals so called, the social and domestic observances, the economies and charities of every-day life. In this sphere her influence has made itself widely felt, and her *works do follow her* in juster views of life and its responsibilities in many homes; in high and noble impulses strengthened, in that every-day practical Christianity which consists in acting and living for the good of others, where formerly there was but the cold expression of a belief only.

"Could there be for woman a worthier aim, or a more exalted sphere? There is a diversity of gifts, and while one devoted woman may feel herself called upon to proclaim the religion of the cross to the dark-skinned children of the Orient, or the red man of our own forests, I question if she will be more truly useful than she who sits at home, and devotes her pen to the conversion of *heathenesse* in our own land. And there is more than enough heathenism, be it said with deepest humility, not among the lowly and ignorant alone, but in the high places of our land. The idolatry of fashion; the shrinking from known duties; the neglect of the better interests of children and their proper instruction and training; the narrow, selfish modes of living which seek only present ease and comfort, and look not to the future which will develop the harvest of all our deeds.

"My own memories of this gifted woman are grateful and tender. In the darkness of a terrible misfortune, in the depths of an almost overwhelming despair, she came to me with such sweet, womanly words of encouragement, and such tender sympathy as I can never forget while life lasts, and pointed me in the way her feet had already trod.

"Such aid as was in her power she gave, and it was not small. But above all I blessed her for her words of truth and faith which directed me to my only true source of help. To me she has seemed ever since, something almost more than mortal woman; and in my imagination I have seen her as the early martyr-Christians saw their saintly woman walk abroad with a visible halo around her head, distilling blessings as she went from the sanctity of her pure life.

"Still untouched by age, beautiful and beloved, death has claimed her. We trust she has but gone to a better home; her quiet, fervent piety, and the exemplary purity and saintliness of her life, forbids every other thought. And so even our sadness has its tender consolation, our grief its tinge of perfect joy."

## COUSIN ALICE'S GRAVE.

I saw her asleep for the last,
Close-clasped in her pale hands a cross;
Her praying and weeping were past,
But we stood in tears for our loss.

The chaplets lay white on her brow,
And lilies lay white on her breast;
Her shroud was as pure as the snow,
But the cross her true beauty expressed.

Life's burdens to bear for the faint
Life's sorrows to share with the sad,
This sweet service made her a saint,
And each rough cross still made her glad.

What else for a sign might be set—
Her wood-cloistered grave to reveal,
Than the cross she is honoring yet—
Though no more its weight she can feel?

The cross at her grave is as white
As that in her hand's icy fold;
That faded, and this will be bright
When the grave yard trees are grown old.

But longer than gleam of the stone
  The light of her life shall endure;
By the cross to us here she was known,
  She lives by the cross with the pure.

W. C. R.

www.ingramcontent.com/pod-product-compliance
Lightning Source LLC
LaVergne TN
LVHW020108110826
845151LV00001B/97

* 9 7 8 1 4 2 5 5 4 3 3 6 5 *